MANCHESTER CITY

MANCHESTER CITY

THE SECRET HISTORY OF A CLUB THAT HAS NO HISTORY

MIKE DEVLIN

AMBERLEY

First published 2015

Amberley Publishing
The Hill, Stroud
Gloucestershire, GL5 4EP

www.amberley-books.com

British Library Cataloguing in Publication Data.
A catalogue record for this book is available from the British Library.

ISBN 978 1 4456 4810 1 (print)
ISBN 978 1 4456 4811 8 (ebook)

Typesetting and Origination by Amberley Publishing.
Printed in the UK.

CONTENTS

ABOUT THIS BOOK

While *Manchester City: The Secret History of a Club That Has No History* contains more true facts than one could shake a rather large pointy inflatable banana at, it is also a work of fiction – which is probably logical for a history of a club that has no history. It's the history as told at matches, pubs and bars between us fans as we passed age-old stories around, laughing and joking and swearing about it. Almost like that 'whisper game' we played as kids, where by the time the message gets to you it has been distorted somewhat. I say this now, so that as you turn each page you will discover that this is a book only a hardened City fan could have written.

I, of course, love my club, but, as every good City fan has always done, taking the piss is in the blood (not literally of course as that would be a rather serious medical condition), and there's a lot of that throughout this book. In fact, there is actually only one real word-for-word direct quote in the book ... see if you can find it.

It is not intended to be an all-knowing encyclopedia of every single event to have ever happened at the club, but one that begins with the birth of football to the world and then covers the major events throughout every decade of the club, along with plenty of quirky happenings (this is all about Manchester City, after all), and plenty of facts and figures thrown in haphazardly.

Kick back, learn and laugh about the greatest football club in all the land and world: Manchester City.

All opinions contained in this book are mine and proffered out of a genuine affection for the game, the club, the owners, the fans, and all those players lovingly referenced.

ABOUT THE AUTHOR

Mike Devlin, a life-long Manchester City fan, who started writing officially for the club in 2013 and founded the award-winning mcfcforum.com in 2010, decided that the history of his beloved club although well documented, was not exactly to his liking – it was just far too serious.

After completing his debut comedic sci-fi novel, *Smith*, he decided to embark on a journey of putting this correct, and what you have in your hands is the result (after the lawyers had removed and censored about half of it). Of course, this is not to say that all others before him have been wrong, just that they haven't been right.

Obviously, the author must have been doing something correct, as Manchester City FC asked him to blog on their official site in the exact same manner this book is written in – only in a much less sweary manner I might add (City censors, huh?).

Born and raised in Manchester, he now lives in Germany with his wife and son, and now the three of them are collectively trying to turn the whole country sky blue.

This book is dedicated to all Citizens who truly knew what it meant to support and follow a club when all common sense told you, you shouldn't. Of course, that doesn't really apply today, does it?

CTWD

Gary says*: 'Bloody good book is this: I'm in it!'
(*Obviously this is one of those fiction bits I mentioned earlier)

You Have the Following to Blame for the Existence of This Book

Gary James, the City historian, for telling me to go for it when I first explained to him what my idea was. Michael O'Keefe for helping out with 'written Irish'; Manchester City FC for allowing me to publish my historical nonsense to millions of City fans on their official site throughout the 2013/14 season. Mcfcforum.com for putting up with me going on about it. My followers on Twitter (which of course you can join in with @BlueWolf1894), who were insistent that they'd buy a copy of this book if I ever finished it. My wife for simply putting up with me and for all her help. Gareth Roberts for his advice and John Stanhope for helping with the title of this book.

A FOREWORD BY REVD ARTHUR CONNELL

I did t'ink it was fierce quare when I was initially asked by d'aut'or to scribble an introduction to dis tome; after all I've been dead well over 100 years – t'was 24th of February 1899, in Southport (lovely aul spot it was, to be sure). But, after some humming and hawing, I said dat alt'ough dying can be a bit of a pain in da arse, I shouldn't let being buried in da ground for a century or so get in da way of me spinning a few yarns.

Sure t'was pretty obvious I had some catching up to do with da history of St Mark's … Lord forgive me, I mean, Manchester City, and so I sat down with dis wonderful book your holding at da moment. Merciful hour wasn't it an awful shock to me when I found out dat my beloved football club is now owned and in da hands of Arabs, but, in turn, 'tis a small mercy dat at least dey aren't de Cat'olics.

It seems the aul club has come a long way since I last saw it, and sure wasn't I in an awful state when I found out dat Newton Heath have had several years of good fortune. But how much debt did ya say them gom's have? Jaysus, Mary, and Joseph! Dat's a lot. Still haven't a notion why da fans wear da Norwich City kit.

Still, I see we're after getting a bit of luck and sure isn't it a sight to behold, 'cause my beloved Manchester City are winning t'ings and known t'roughout de world, even in places as far afield as Glasgow. Evidently, da Manchester City fans have been God-fearing people – sure how else could you explain da mighty support?

I'm after learning a grand amount of new facts from dis deadly book – who knew t'em Germans weren't a nice aul sort? But I would like to point out dat young wan of mine, Anna, was a pain in me arse; always taking me whisky away, she was. Well ya can't take it away from me now, can ya, ya aul biddy?

IN THE BEGINNING –
THE BIRTH OF FOOTBALL

There is some debate as to who, and maybe just as importantly, when, football first began in England.[1] After all, with football taking up so much of our lives, it must have been around forever, right? As luck would have it, research does indeed point to a very early beginning for the world's game.

Excavations in the Cheddar Gorge, in dirt carbon-dated to around 20,000BC, revealed what one expert described as 'caved-in skulls with foot-shaped indentations', possibly pointing to the first ever rudimentary football. However, it wasn't until several bladders were found from numerous animal species that the initial conclusion of skulls being used as balls had in fact been incorrect, and instead pointed to the birth of football hooliganism – although experts have been quick to point out that these nomadic peoples had more than likely come from France.

However, there is much evidence that points to games involving balls and feet being played all over the world – China, America (long before it was called America – go ask the original inhabitants, they'll tell you), Greece, Rome, and of course Egypt. But, as any (xenophobic) purist of the game will tell you, football was an English invention, so we'll stick with that then.

Fast forward a little bit (actually a lot), and football was beginning to spread like wildfire during the 1300s, however, the game being played was vastly different to what is played today, in that the players involved had no respect for the rules and sporadic moments of violence occasionally erupted. Oh, and teams consisted of around 300 per side.

These games were also played on a 'pitch', which essentially encompassed an entire town, so it wasn't out of the ordinary to have games that lasted all day, particularly when a player who owned the ball remembered they had to be somewhere else and went home, taking it with them without informing anyone. Happy times.

Obviously the aristocracy of the time frowned upon the whole affair (even though they themselves actually played football – Mary, Queen of Scots even wrote about it, in a 'do as I say, not as I do' style), not least because one could not be seen allowing one's subjects doing anything that was considered to be fun. Even William Shakespeare got in on the act[2] when he used the actual word 'football' in the lesser-known play ridiculing the game, 'Stepney 3 The Abbey of Saint-Josse 2'. As such, there were several instances of the game being banned leading to underground leagues, which were not very successful due to it being very dark down there. Still, football had already made its mark and within time it always managed to return, resulting in another small hamlet being demolished during match days.

During the seventeenth century, leading British public schools adopted the game as their own, attempting to instil a modicum of class into the proceedings. However, each devised their own rules, which although thought acceptable for them, started to create problems when they played against each other – most notably when Georgie Thompson was seen catching the ball during one such Eton and Harrow game only to have a fist planted firmly in his face with both sides arguing that under the rules both were allowed. Something had to be done.

In 1862, Cambridge University devised a new set of rules that could be universally adopted – eleven men a side, a standard goal size (admittedly 20 inches high and 118 inches wide) and an offside rule, as even the Industrial Revolution hated a goalhanger.

Fun Things To Do

Relive the 1700s and 1800s by gathering some friends round and tell them you have invented a new game with a ball, then pull each one aside and give out conflicting rules. Watch the hilarity ensue at kick-off.

Then, in 1863, a group of men, ironically known as the Football Association, conceived the official rule book. It consisted of rudimentary laws, stating what was and what wasn't allowed and based upon the laws created the previous year. However, the offside rule was to their disliking as it was too easily understood and therefore had to be changed, which soon accounted for seventeen pages of the twenty-three-page rule book.

But not all were particularly happy with these rules, as they readily objected to players being allowed to catch the ball after one bounce, saying that it was 'uncivilised'; they also used this phrase when discovering that you could no longer boot someone viciously.

'Catch the ball and run, sans a trifle kicking to the gonads? We are men, by George! We will not stand for these shenanigans!'

But the FA stood their ground and did much finger-pointing, resulting in the rules being adopted, or at least they were by the clubs who wanted to play under the FA. Those who didn't played under an entirely different set of rules formulated by the twenty-six-team Sheffield Association (noted for its extreme popularity, as is evident today by its worldwide status of the association to belong to – Barcelona FC has been desperate to get into it for years).

It wasn't until 1881 that the FA became the force in football they craved and virtually all were unified under one banner.[3] But a year earlier a woman stepped into the fray – for she had had a vision from God...

Challenge

Why is American Football not called Handball? See if you can find out.

A Manchester City Fan of the 1300s Has His Say

Name: Scrogg, son of Scrogg.
Age: Umm…
First City game ever attended: When the priory 'ung Mad Melvin.
Priory 1 Mad Melvin 0.

Manchester what? Football? Oh, no, Sir, ne'er play that; the King 'as banned it, Sir. The King says we 'ave to be ready to fight them crazy French peoples. I am more of a mud man, can't beat a good bit o' mud. Not sure what yer could do with it in a war though.

Oh, yer not a sheriff? Ah, well that be different then, although a half-penny might jog me memory, Sir.

Much obliged to yer, Sir. Now then, football. Oh, yes, everyone plays it – well, them that don't be 'aving the plague that is, can't kick a ball if yer leg's gonna fall off, can yer?

But yer got to go to the forest. Mind yer, them trees get in the way sometimes, that an' good mud is a bit lackin' over there.

So what's this Manchester City? An entire city playing football? Even the Bishop? No Sir, never met an Ian Bishop. Is 'e in the mud business?

So, cities play other cities? 'Ow's that goin' to work? I knew someone who went to Stafford 40 miles away and that took 'im two whole days to get there.

The people pay to watch? Don't mean to be disrespectful, Sir, but I reckon yer've been at the ale a bit too much.

Imagine? 'Fraid I don't 'ave much of an imagination – most of me time is taken up with mud. Can I interest yer in a bucket o' mud? Perfect for making bricks an' all sorts of things, wouldn't recommend eating it though – at least not this type.

Fair enough, Sir, but if yer change yer mind, just let me know – an' good luck with that Manchester Cities thing.

---

1 Actually, there isn't any debate, but we'll pretend there is, otherwise this chapter will be going nowhere fast.
2 LOL – I made a funny.
3 A dark and foreboding banner, where those under it put their fingers in their ears and said, 'La, la, la, I'm not listening.'

MANCHESTER CITY IS BORN FROM THE STREETS OF ... WELL, MANCHESTER

It was the late nineteenth century – 1880 to be exact – and the city of Manchester was a grimy greasehole where law and order was best described as 'not done very well'.

The Industrial Revolution that had begun in the city and spread worldwide had put Manchester firmly on the map, resulting in many to come to this place to find employment at some degrading and unfulfilling workplace (not at all like today).

Trouble was that there were many who possessed the common sense and skill of a cabbage, so for these men their days were spent drinking and wandering around aimlessly, picking random fights and rogering anything that moved (again, not at all like today).

This turn of events had, however, not gone unnoticed by a certain Anna Connell of St Mark's church in West Gorton, who had taken it upon herself to propose that the local men needed something better to do than beating 10 tons of shit out of each other. She even pointed to the passage of scripture in Thessalonians 1 5:7, that states:

> For they that sleep sleep in the night; and they that be drunken are drunken in the night; and they that are buggered up the jacksie will more than likely be relatively upset during the night.

Suggesting to the churchwardens, William Beastow and Thomas Goodbehere, she surmised that the men's daily routine would be better served via the church organising games in the manner of a new and upcoming sport called football.

And so it became so – the first and only club to have been formed by a woman. Yes, I know! I find it as hard to believe as you do, but that's what history says. So the next time your woman complains about you watching the game, you just remind her of ol' Anna. Put that in your pipe and smoke it. And while you're at it, make me some dinner, woman, I'm hungry.

Author's Side Note, Which for Some Strange Reason has been Placed Slap-Bang in the Middle

There is actually some (well okay, actually a lot of) evidence pointing towards Anna having absolutely nothing at all to do with the formation of our football club, but rather claiming it was the male officials of St Mark's church. However, that would mean Manchester City is just like every other football club in existence, and neither would you be able to use the 'put that in your pipe and smoke it' line, which, obviously, simply will not do.

So, the team was named St Mark's (wonder how long it took her to come up with that name?), and the men finally had something to do. The first game was set up and went off without much fuss, until they realised upon arriving that there was no one to play against and that they would actually need some opponents; something that Anna had failed to realise initially (she's a woman, y'see).

Once the confusion that originally had occurred during their first 'game' had been solved, the men who signed up for the team of St Mark's spent their days practising this so-called football, while being preached to about the error of their ways. So successful was Ms Connell's approach, that it was reported that sexual assault in the area dropped by a staggering 37 per cent virtually overnight, although there were some who attributed this to the fact that the men were too knackered to 'get it up', due to the intensive short-passing and 3-2-4-1 system she had introduced.

It is worthy to note that from 1875, up until the incarnation of the St Mark's football team, the church had played cricket, which of course they had been ridiculed for by the nearby St Peter's for playing a game fit for pansies. To this day, St Peter's still holds their annual tiddlywinks tournament, and they are very proud of it thank you very much.

So the history that was to become, funnily enough, the history of Manchester City, began in the year of 1880. Now although we learned that it was a woman who created our beloved club (maybe, but probably not), we see William Beastow stepping forward to disagree completely (who obviously hasn't read the side note in the middle). It was him who had come up with the original idea to create a cricket team five years earlier, and it is he who is regarded to have come up with the initial idea of creating a football team. He was also quoted in the weekly church minute meetings, as saying, 'A woman? A woman in charge of football? No good can come of it, Bertrand.'[1]

However, regardless of who was the true founder, Beastow recruited hardworking honest men from the local ironworks factory, whereas Anna Connell recruited those who were, shall we say, scum, and the very first recorded game using these men was against a Baptist Church from Macclesfield on 13 November. The final score is unknown, but it can only be presumed that St Mark's were awesome and they won like 85-0 or something.

Gary says: 'Strong of character was good ol' Anna Connell; a firm foundation on which to build a mighty football club.'

Due to literacy and numeracy not being practised particularly well, teams were made up of twelve, instead of the usual eleven, although this might have had something to do with the 'Fatty' McTavish twins, who always insisted on being a part of everything, even though they were less use than a venereal disease.

Newspapers of the day began their talent of not being able to report the news correctly by calling this new team either St Mark's or West Gorton, and changing it on a day-to-day basis. Unknown to all, this bad reporting would go unchecked throughout the history of 'news'papers up to and including the present day.[2]

In the 'season' of 1881/82, St Mark's met for the very first time a team that was to become their arch enemy – Newton Heath. So apt was their name, that it lent itself to the name 'Heathens', which they have been doing their utmost to live up to ever since. The game was played at their new home at Kirkmanshulme Cricket Club, thereby finally being able to show the locals what a proper sport was. Again, the final score is unknown, but, again, we can only presume it was an embarrassing result for the Heathens, who more than likely ran home crying like little girls.

In 1882, the cricket club (presumably fed up with being shown up by the manly footballers and also rather pissed that their beautiful cricket pitch now resembled a bomb site), asked St Mark's to leave and moved to Queen's Road, a little further east along Hyde Road. However, some of the cricketers, presumably fearing for their own manliness, joined this new football club, and so the men from the ironworks, the street and the cricket club made up the squad of St Mark's.

It was during this time, up to 1884, that St Mark's football club underwent major changes, the biggest of which was to officially change their name to West Gorton (including moving once more, to Pink Bank Lane – presumably to appease the local growing gay community). In fact, the senior church figures were indeed instrumental to these changes because they wanted to create a proper professional side. It was also mentioned by Beastow that he'd had one or two problems from Ms Connell. 'What did I tell you, Bertrand? She's a woman! What the dickens she is doing out of the kitchen, I will never know, my dear chap. Someone ought to take a rod to her!'

At the end of 1884, a massive riot occurred between Gorton and Openshaw[3] and it became evident that the area desperately needed something to belong to. The club joined the Manchester FA and Beastow presented the players with a brand new kit – black with a white Maltese Cross on it.[4]

The 1880s were very pivotal in the growth of West Gorton, as once again they found themselves moving home and sat and watched the Heathens start to win things like the Manchester Cup. West Gorton wanted to be a part of this and they felt that they had to return to their roots by returning to an area they were more familiar with (and where the hookers were also cheaper).

They moved to Bennett Street changing their name yet again to Ardwick, and with a brand new pitch their opening fixture on 10 September 1887 against Salford FC was announced. Alas, Salford FC didn't actually show up – it was half-price night on Sackville Street.

Ardwick had never managed to reach a final of the Manchester Cup, but in April 1891 it finally happened. Playing in their new colours of blue (which had been introduced in 1887), they took on the evil empire, Newton Heath. Suffice to say, the pure of heart won that day 1-0, although it should have been 2-0, but the Heathens objected to Ardwick's second goal and it was disallowed.[5]

1887 was also the year that West Gorton moved to Hyde Road, a plot of land owned by a railway company but used by the local rent boys. To celebrate this fact, a small part of the stadium was named the 'Boy's Stand'. Additionally, the makers of the 1985 movie, *Brewster's Millions*, paid homage to Hyde Road when they featured a freight train moving through the baseball field, mirroring what happened frequently at Ardwick's new home.

Using the success of the Manchester Cup, Ardwick applied to join the 'Big Boys' in the football league. They failed, but so too did the Heathens. Ardwick did eventually end up in the football league in 1892, but in Division Two. The Heathens, however, somehow managed to worm their way in to Division One but didn't stay there for very long. How they managed this in the first place, we will never know, as Ardwick were a much bigger club, and were far more well-known – not suggesting anything underhanded went on though.

Although Ardwick was now establishing itself as a proper club, there were concerns that they could no longer afford to keep operating if half their revenue was being spent on cheap hookers and booze. But on Monday 16 April 1894, Ardwick cast aside its old ways and became Manchester City FC.

Not wanting to completely forget Ardwick, the club voted for a new motto, and the winner was, 'Even in our own ashes, live our wanted fires', which only narrowly beat, 'Don't touch Betty Swabble, she's a dirty minger'.[6]

It is interesting to note that at the same time that Ardwick were changing their name to that of Manchester City (officially meaning 'team of the Manchester area'), the Heathens wanted to change their name to that of Manchester FC. They were explicitly told not to by the League due a legal objection by the local rugby club, who were called Manchester at that time. There was only ever to be just one official Manchester club in the area and they weren't it.[7]

Initially, there were some problems with some of the Ardwick players who didn't want the club to be transformed into something shiny and new, with some saying that the name had changed so often they didn't have a bloody clue who they were playing for. 'Well, we'll set up our own Ardwick club, and we'll be awesome and amazing and stuff,' some said – as history records show that went well, didn't it?

The Football League, however, needed convincing that Manchester City should be allowed to take Ardwick's place in the division – we had no money, barely a fit XI, but we did (because it was Ardwick's) have a brand new stadium, and the FA had already said that City were the official team of Manchester, so how could they not agree to it?

Quite easily, as it turned out. But with some expert bullshit from club secretary, Joshua Parlsby, at a meeting with the FA, they actually said yes, believing that Manchester City would take decades to establish themselves at the top of the table, thereby not upsetting the true giants of the game like Sheffield Wednesday and Everton.

In the guise of the brand new and very shiny Manchester City, the club kicked off its first season away to Bury (losing 4-2) on 1 September, with virtually a brand new squad. Only Fred Dyer had survived from the ashes of Ardwick to feature that day; every other player had been brought in during the summer in what the local media were coining as 'ADUG'.[8]

1894 also saw the introduction of football's biggest star of the day – Billy Meredith. He would have signed for Bolton Wanderers from Northwich Victoria, but incredibly (in a 'Those four Liverpool lads can't sing or play, and will get nowhere in life' manner) they believed he wasn't worth it, so in stepped City and snapped him up. Trouble was, it took a year for Meredith to break his habit of going down the pits – in his blood y'see – as he would play his match and then run off back down some grimy hole where he was happiest. It wasn't until City turned him into a professional footballer with a good wage that he realized that perhaps sitting in a hole all day was probably not the greatest way to spend one's time.

Something strange happened at the beginning of the 1895/96 season concerning the FA Cup and Manchester City. The previous season City decided not to bother with the competition at all for some reason, but then re-entered it in 1895 and were to play QPR. But then at the last minute, they withdrew from the competition (as they had done before in the 1890/91 season) and no one knows why. Around the same time, the previous winners, Aston Villa, had the trophy on show in Birmingham, someone stole it and it was never seen again. In 1958, a man named Harry Burge was said to have said that he had stolen it to make counterfeit coins, but I am not buying that perfectly acceptable story for a second. Why enter a competition when you already have your hands on the prize?

At the close of the nineteenth century, Manchester City were promoted to Division One, but Anna Connell could not share in their triumphs for she had left the area, knowing that her work had been completed by giving the local men something to be a part of, that didn't involve anal sex down the back of an alley.

Towards the end of the century, the Football League, which up until then had a system of election to determine who (if anyone) went up and down a league, were forced to change the rules after a 0-0 result between Burnley and Stoke in 1898. Both sides needed a draw and so decided to simply pass the ball around without either side even having a shot on goal – at one point, the two opposing 'keepers went off to the pub for an hour, and the Stoke backline performed a Gilbert and Sullivan piece for their travelling fans. From the 1898/99 season the League introduced automatic promotion and relegation for the top team in Division Two and the bottom team in Division One. The reason this was so important was because, as already said, City were promoted into the top tier and they became the first club to do so under these new rules – was this a conspiracy to get the Citizens into Division One? Or simply to piss off Anna Connell now that she was no longer in the country? Score one for Beastow, methinks.

God Bless the *Manchester City*, and All Who Sail in Her, No. 1

How do you know how awesome you are? When a brand new ship is launched and named after you, that's how. The *Manchester City* was a big ship – the biggest ever on the Manchester Ship Canal – and all were amazed by her, except for Liverpudlians who weren't impressed every time she sailed through Liverpool, but who then rejoiced when she was scrapped in 1929. We'll be back Scousers, we'll be back ...

Happy Birthday Manchester City!
16 April

9-0 *v.* Burton in 1898

Notable Players of the Late Nineteenth Century

James Cairns, 1892–94
The early 1890s was a time when literally anyone could make an appearance for a football club. Only one foot? Not a problem. Blind? How do you fancy the left-back position? Not so for Jimmy Cairns. After signing with Ardwick FC, he had to wait eighteen months and a change of manager before he could get a competitive game, but was then never picked again. Maybe Newton Heath will give me game time, thought Cairns, but after signing with them in 1894, he had to wait seven months to step out on to the pitch, and as with Ardwick, was never picked again. The Mighty Cairns hung up his boots for good in 1895 – and you thought Christian Negouai was bad.

Joe O'Brien, 1893
Joe's dream was to become an Ardwick FC hero, but after Joshua Parlsby only picked him twice and then permanently dropped him, he swore revenge. 119 years later, his namesake Shaun O'Brien attempted to stop the building of the new academy by selling small plots of land to Manchester United fans. Oh, Joshua, why!

Walter Bowman, 1893–99

The Football League's first ever non-British person was Canadian Bowman's claim to fame. Once City discovered he wasn't French Canadian, they welcomed him with open arms.

Billy Meredith, 1894–1906
Billy became the fifth highest goalscorer for the club, but it was said that he could have claimed the No. 1 spot had he not refused to always play while drinking ale from his favourite tankard.

Charlie Williams, 1894–1902
The first 'keeper to ever score a goal in a league game, Charlie was a formidable shot-stopper who would take no prisoners when confronted with attacking opposition.
Plays: 232
Confirmed kills: 13

Billie Gillespie, 1897–1905
After being forced to change the spelling of his first name by Meredith, who had trademarked 'Billy', Billie settled in comfortably. He was the front man in City's much heralded 4-1-3-1-0-1 formation, being found so far up the pitch he often had to pay to get back into the ground.

Jimmy Ross, 1898–1901
Ross was different to most other professional players of his day, in so far as that he was actually a decent footballer and he took it very seriously. Upon hearing of the Football League's decision to impose a maximum wage of £4 a week and to stop all bonuses, he joined a group of players and formed the Association Footballer's Union so he could get the £10 a week he wanted. Both he and they failed. As it is always better dead than (in the) red, he decided to die in 1902.

The Maltese Falcon, 1898
Technically not a player, as the Falcon was City's first attempt at a club mascot. Sadly, the Falcon only lasted for two games after being introduced in 1898, as the local hobo who had been employed to play the role, defecated on the penalty spot during a match versus Everton.

A Manchester City Fan of the 1890s Has His Say

Name: George Beshall

Age: Dunno

First City game ever attended: Are you a copper? 'Cause I swear on me mam's life I 'ave always paid to get int't see a game.

Well, it's grand, innit? Not so sure about that Anna woman though – it ain't right y'see, what wiv her being a woman an' all. 'Ow can she be tellin' men 'ow t' kick a ball about? Never seen her kick it, now 'ow's that gonna work? Anyway, she's doin' Lord's work i'nt she? An' that's gotta be worth somethin', right?

Are you sure you ain't a copper? Oh, right, if you say so, Guv'nor. Me favourite player? Oh, I don't rightly know about that. Don't know the names, y'see. Although, me mate did go for a try-out, 'e's good wiv a ball, 'cause we is always 'aving a kickabout after work up at mill. Thing is though, 'e stole half a pound of butter from the kitchen in the church – he said 'im and his missus needed it for somethin', dunno what though, 'cause neither of them can cook.

But, yeah, they caught him, di'nt they? Silly bugger. Not seen him for a couple of days now, suspect coppers 'ave 'im locked up somewhere.

Hey, that Taff player is alright, i'nt he? Tight bleeder wiv 'is money though, wouldn't buy me a pint, would 'e? There's somethin' shifty about 'im, but 'e can't 'alf kick a ball.

Look mate, I promised Bill I'd meet 'im down by canal for somethin' … huh? … No, mate, it's nothin' shifty … I just gotta … You'll never take me alive, copper!

---

1 See Karren Brady for further proof.
2 Go on, I dare you to prove to me that I am wrong. Yeah, that's what I thought.
3 Once more, not at all like today.
4 Some noted that it was also very German in style – not that anyone minded, because, as every Englishman knew, Germans were very nice people and would never do something silly like start a war.
5 Cheating, surrounding and harassing the ref? Them? Well, I never…
6 No, I have no idea what it really means either.
7 HA HA HA HA HA HA HA HA HA HA HA!
8 Acquiring Daring Unusual Geniuses.

MANCHESTER CITY COME TO THE RESCUE OF MANCHESTER UNITED

At the turn of the century, the club were nicknamed the Breweries or the Brewerymen, primarily because they were essentially owned by a brewery – this seemed like a very sensible moniker considering that for the last twenty years most of the players were heavily intoxicated each day by 9:15 a.m. (they had, during the 1890s, previously been nicknamed the Slags, due to the local coal mines owning them).[1] What was also very apt about this was that from 1887 to 1896 there were no changing rooms at Hyde Road, so the players got changed into their kits at the Hyde Road Hotel, which was, yes, a pub (owned by said brewery). This would also explain the odd occasional heavy home defeat due to the 2-hour happy hour that began at 1 p.m. on a Saturday.

In 1902, Newton Heath were beginning to feel the burden of pushing themselves to be a part of Division One in the Football League, which of course serves them right. Ironically, had they entered into Division Two with City (not that City really had any choice in the matter) they would have had time to grow, but their impatience of several years earlier would seal their fate. They had survived in Division One for two seasons, only to drop down and join St Mark's/West Gorton/Ardwick/ – whatever the hell they were calling themselves that week – just as they were transforming into Manchester City FC. They languished (as did City) in Division Two for the next nine seasons, only to discover that they had not only ran out of money but had run out of borrowed money too. It was also rumoured that they had been spending even more money than City on local hookers and booze – an exceptional feat in itself.

The Heathens attempted to raise as much money as was possible in a bazaar in the city centre (the club owed well over £2,000), and although Mrs Miggins' pies proved to be very popular, the much-touted 'how many ferrets do I have down my pants?' proved to be a disaster when the gentleman who was to run the event had part of his testicles bitten off within the first 5 minutes.

Quite staggeringly, Manchester City attempted to come to the rescue. Even though they (rightly) believed that they were the official club of the area, they knew that the city was big enough for two major teams and so the directors sportingly handed over £11 (£1,000 today) of their own money to Newton Heath.

Gary says: 'Well that's just plain embarrassing isn't it? Maybe when it's all over we can cheer them all up by giving them a huge WELCOME TO MANCHESTER CITY.'

Alas, it was too little too late for the club and the heavy burden of debt became too much, with the amount of money the directors of the club had managed to raise at the bazaar only being a little more than to pay for the costs of said bazaar (and recompense for the ferret entertainer). The owners of the club had previously only been interested in getting as much money for themselves as possible.[2]

However, from this, and with the support of Manchester City, the Heathens became Manchester United.[3] As a side note, they had been relegated from Division One after losing against Liverpool FC; obviously today's generation of United fans have never forgiven the Scousers for this.

Oh, and they decided on the name of 'United', not because they wanted to be 'as one', but because Sheffield United were awesome and they hoped that stupid people wouldn't be able to tell the difference and so get some extra fans. Hmm … Manchester United reckoning their own fans are stupid?

So, before the summer of 1902, Manchester United was born; although rumour has it that the creation of the club rested purely on the shoulders of a Saint Bernard dog. The dog in question was owned by the captain, who gave it to the daughter of the man who was to become the new owner – J. H. Davies – in return for several thousand pounds of investment.

Manchester City, created by a woman; Manchester United, created by a bitch.

That season, when the two teams met, they ended in a 1-1 draw and a 0-2 win for United, but at least City managed to finish top of the League, gaining promotion into Division One. While this was all very awesome and the like, something evil was stirring in the distance.

---

1 And because they were heavily intoxicated by 9.15 a.m.
2 Obviously they would learn from this mistake and never again have owners who were only in it for themselves while skimming money off the top.
3 Still heathens though.

THE FA'S 'HATE CAMPAIGN' AGAINST MANCHESTER CITY

When the Football League began, it was one of those cutesy things; something to be looked upon with love, and with much 'ah'-ing'. This made the FA very happy indeed, much like when a parent looks upon their young child as he begins to figure out that his face isn't his mouth when it comes to eating. What didn't make the FA happy, however, was Manchester City.

You see, City were starting to look like a very big and competent side. They were right in the middle of a large metropolis and were going about their business professionally – exactly the sort of thing the FA did not want.[1] City were no longer a child and were growing very quickly, too quickly. The FA Cup win of 1903/04 was evidence of this ... apparently. Manchester City FC was only ten years old, and as such had no right to be crowned champions after such a short space of time – after all, what would older established clubs think? Can't have them being upset now, can we?

In their 'infinite wisdom', the FA deemed that the club must be up to no good, because their success couldn't simply be put down to buying good players and getting the most out of them, and so, during the entire off-season of 1904, their books were given a good seeing to by officials to find something they could charge them with. They found absolutely nothing. Or did they?

As it turned out, two players signed from Glossop had forged receipts, and as they dug deeper the FA discovered that City had gone over the £10 sign-on fee threshold for each player.[2] It was City's argument that they should be able to pay their players what they wanted. It was the FA's argument that players should get what they were told and like it. A stalemate began. Actually, that's a lie, because the FA rained down fire and brimstone upon them, and then did lots of finger pointing and clearing of throats excessively loudly.

The club was fined £250, and Hyde Road ordered to be closed for two games, with one of the players suspended for a season, three directors banned for three years, the finance director banned for life, and the club mascot taken round the back and given a good kicking.

Despite the FA's actions, City finished third that season in the League and second in the local 'best tasting pie' competition, although it was suspected that the eventual winner – a Mrs Thornhill – was sleeping with at least three of the judges.

Of course, Manchester City didn't need any help from the FA to remove their own players, because they were quite good at doing it themselves. In 1902, David Jones was playing in a practice game when he slipped and fell onto a piece of glass, resulting in a cut to his knee. The City medical team (basically a guy with a bottle of whisky) deduced he was fine, but several days later Jones was dead due to an infection in the wound. Then, in 1904, they gave a trial to a man by the name of Harry Kay in a reserve game; he ended up scoring four goals and the City board realized they had a massive star on their hands. After the game he was paraded about and shown off by the club to the onlooking public who clapped and cheered. The police, however, were not as impressed and immediately moved in and placed Kay under arrest – he was a known army deserter.

Anyway, the FA, after coming down hard upon City in 1904, set about to open a can of whoop-ass on them, for City were still perceived as being 'too big for their Edwardian, Louis-heel, jet-beaded shoes.'

It all started with a game against Aston Villa in the closing stage of the 1904/05 season. City lost the game 3-2, but Sandy Turnbull was violently attacked by Villa players and staff after the game and the police had to protect the Citizens to enable them to leave the ground.

Of course, City reported this, and the FA looked into it, and then delivered their findings; Turnbull was suspended for a month.[3] They didn't stop there however, and went on to accuse Billy Meredith of attempting to bribe Villa so that City could win the game.

Villa, you see, had 'gotten into bed' with the FA, and the FA seemed to be afraid that City were becoming too big and too professional, and also refused to bend over and squeal like a pig.

Gary says: 'Bottled it. That's what the FA have done. We had a deal in place, but if they can't stand the soup, they should get out of the bedroom.'

Billy Meredith protested vehemently saying, 'I'll see you down in the val-leys', but was immediately banned.[4] The FA then sent an auditor to the club to check on everything (again), to find something – anything – because City were evil and danced on the local graves at night, chanting to Beelzebub. City were also told they were not allowed to support Meredith in any manner, be it wages, advice or his one-man show in Gorton where he performed interpretive dance.[5] Meredith was a little upset by this and changed his story, saying that City had told him to offer the bribe. This was what the FA were waiting for, and a few months later, the aforementioned can of whoop-ass was indeed opened.

The club was charged with over-paying players across the board, and a total of seventeen current and former players, plus directors, were suspended for almost a year, and fines of over £1,000 were issued. No football club has ever suffered as much as City did that day.[6]

Fun Things To Do

Pretend to be the head of the FA for a day at home, and see how many members of your household you can piss off.

Manchester United eventually ended up signing Meredith along with three other City players and went on to climb the table because of them, where before they might have entered total obscurity. City on the other hand, struggled, but managed to remain in the top-flight despite what the FA had done to them.

Billie Gillespie, one of the fined players, point-blank refused to pay anything to the FA and simply buggered off to America instead – the FA still have him listed as their 'second most wanted man' (No. 1 being Graham Taylor), even though he died in Massachusetts in 1942.

The following season, with most of the players now absent or on the run from the FA, Manchester City introduced so many new players that Harry Newbould, the manager, called everyone 'oy, you'. During their first match, City ended up with only six players on the field come the full-time whistle, losing five to heat exhaustion. While this resulted in them losing 1-4, they were not much better with a full squad as was proven in their next game against Everton, losing 1-9.

Yet during 1908/09, City's home form was superb – only four teams won more and five teams scored more. The debacle of the mid-1900s was finally over.

Actually, no, no it wasn't. Despite being awesome at home, they were positively diabolical away and City finished nineteenth – they were starting the 1910s back in Division Two. Division Two was to prove to be a home from home for City over the coming decades, and to prove this point to all and sundry, City hold the record for most titles won in the second tier of English football.[7]

Happy Birthday Manchester City!
16 April

2-0 *v.* West Bromich Albion
4-0 *v.* Small Heath
3-0 *v.* Everton
I could get used to this.

Notable Players of the 1900s

Frank Hesham, 1900

Hesham was the Anelka of his day – not in the prolific goalscoring sense of the word, but in the 'I must play for as many different clubs as possible' sense of the word.

As soon as he realised he had already played a couple of games for City in 1896, he left after his first game to go to Crewe Alexander for a day or two, before going to Accrington Stanley, then Stoke, then Leyton, then Oldham, then Preston.

Howard Harvey, 1900/01

Harvey was playing for Port Vale when he caught the eye of Manchester City. He caught their eye because he was scoring for them like it was going out of fashion. Evidently moving to City was not fashionable.

Sandy Turnbull, 1902–06

Turnbull was one of many players who were suspended from playing at City by the FA. Evidently he got the bug for this sort of thing, because he ended up getting a lifetime ban in 1915 for match-fixing. Serves him right for going to Manchester United then.

Billy Lot Jones, 1903–19

The most notable thing about Billy was that he was not implicated in the payment scandal, but this was probably due to him being paid in lumps of coal.

Irvine Thornley, 1904–12

In the Football League's early years, football truly was a man's game. What constitutes as a foul in today's era would have been considered to be perfectly acceptable 100 years ago. So quite what Thornley did to get sent off in almost every game he played in is anyone's guess.

George Dorsett, 1905–12

In 1905, the UK yearly wage for your average Joe was around £60. Dorsett arrived at City from Norwich for £450. Manchester City, ruining football since the 1900s.

Tom Holford, 1908–14

Holford picked up the nickname 'Dirty Tommy', during his playing days. He used to play for Stoke, so there's no surprise there then.

Patsy Hendren, 1909

Patsy was not a woman, just a man with a woman's name. He was also a full-time cricketer.

A Manchester City Fan of the 1900s Has His Say

Name: Pete Stickle
Age: 22
First City game ever attended: Derby County at home (we won!)

Oh, I love me the City, although that FA fing, don't, do they? Who'd they fink they are? How much was it they said they paid? Huh? More than £10? Each? Bloody hell! If I had that kind of money, I'd take my Susan on a luxury week's holiday in North Wales, and treat her like a Princess. She's my sweetheart. Oh, and I would buy one of them new wireless radio fings – they say you can hear music and such like on them!

City? Well, they're doing alright, aren't they? In Division One and sticking two fingers up at that FA. United are doing alright as well, I've been to a few of their games, too – well, they do have half of our players, don't they? So it's almost like watching the same bleedin' side, only in a different colour.

I would like one of their shirts though … City's mate, not United's – my Susan says red don't look good on me.

Hopes? I dunno. It's a football team, it's just somefing to do on a Saturday with my mates. Don't really matter, does it?

Anyway mate, I gotta go meet Susan, I reckon I might even get to hold her hand tonight!

---

1 This would not always be the case, but we have plenty of time to get to that.
2 Bugger.
3 He was accused of headbutting fists and his face being too tough for the wimpy Brummies.
4 This is what all Welshmen say to everything.
5 Six showings a day, with half-price admission for all showings before 2 p.m.
6 Portsmouth of 2010 really did their best to beat this one. Bless them.
7 Premier League titles, pah!

WAR! WHAT IS IT GOOD FOR?
ANSWERS ON
A POSTCARD PLEASE

Every now and then, something manages to get in the way of football, and in 1914 it came in the minor inconvenience of a huge global war, which was unfortunate as City had finished fifth and only three points off the champions Everton (back when they had some money). The 1914/15 season actually kicked off as normal, even though the UK was officially at war from 28 July, but this was due to the people reckoning it was nothing more than a storm in a teacup and would be over by the weekend. Even when it was realized that this was no end-of-week kerfuffle, the League continued on, because, well, let's face it, it's football; some things are important y'know.

Additionally, a match between United and Liverpool on Good Friday of that season had been fixed and several players on both sides were banned for life, only to be reinstated after the war due to service for their country. While it was probably much nicer for these players to go to a brutal war than play for either of these two sides, that rigged win for United gave them an extra two points, which without would have seen them relegated to Division Two. Coincidentally, the FA expanded the top division, and the bottom two teams, Chelsea and Arsenal, were allowed to stay. Rig a game and get away with it, pay players too much and, oh, no Sir! Smacked bottoms all round.

The Football League was abandoned at the end of the 1914/15 season and teams began to play in regional leagues instead. During the first year of the war leagues, City finished first, although, during the home match against Liverpool that ended 1-0, George Kay, the Red's manager, objected to City's goal because a sea mine was thrown on to the pitch and it distracted the goalkeeper when the football hit it and proceeded to bounce into the net. Once the war was over, however, the League was re-established and City, for the most part, didn't actually suffer too badly – well, not straight away.

Prior to this, however, City were proving to all around them that they weren't particularly too bright when it came to financial issues. Harry Taylor came on to the market, and Port Vale snapped him up for £30 only to immediately sell him to the Blues for £300, without even kicking a ball for Vale. Just before the outbreak of the First World War, City spent an additional £4,280 on two players, only for them not to be used for five years.[1]

But tragedy was just around the corner for City, just as they were beginning to find themselves as a force in the League. In 1920, the main stand at Hyde Road burned down.[2] Within days, the club had contacted United asking them if they could ground-share at Old Trafford (which by the way was crippling them in debt). United agreed, but wanted excessive amounts of money resulting in City telling them to 'go shove it up your arse, and don't come crying to us if your stadium ever gets bombed'.

City (admittedly with much help from the local Scout troop, who coincidentally had just started a 'rebuild a stadium badge', and had up until that point wondered if they'd ever have the chance to accomplish it), did a patch-up job of the main stand just in time for a home game against their money-grabbing neighbours, which, of course, City won.

It was deemed by the club, however, that they needed a new ground, and a much bigger one too, because they could never fit all the fans in to Hyde Road who wanted to come. So, in 1923, they moved to Maine Road, which was ironic really because the City fans had been singing 'we are City, super City, we are City from Maine Road' since 1897.

Initially, City were to move to the Belle Vue area of East Manchester, but could not find a large enough area, so ended up settling on the formerly named Dog Kennel Road in the very well-to-do and most pleasant and peaceful of places – Moss Side. The road was renamed to Maine Road in the 1870s in support of the Temperance Movement that began in the 1850s in the State of Maine, USA, which had now spread to the UK – obviously they had no idea who was going to move to this area of the city fifty years later.

The original plans had been to create a 120,000 capacity stadium, but when this proved too costly and threatened to eat into the alcohol and party budget (Temperance Movement, seriously?), it was downgraded to a maximum of around 80,000, at a cost of £100,000.

It wasn't all plain sailing to begin with, as it has been said that gypsies were living on the proposed site, who obviously had to be 'relocated'. Unsurprisingly, they were not overly enthused about this, and so they cursed the very ground the stadium was to be built on. This would certainly explain a few things. A mere 300 days later, the 'Wembley of the North' was finished, and City had the finest club stadium in the country.[3] If only the team had matched.

In 1924, the FA did something remarkable; they attempted to make the offside rule a little easier to play with and understood by players, officials and fans alike. Where it had been a 'three opponent' rule, they changed it to a 'two opponent' rule, which is still the current law. What this did was to make it easier to score, to which Frank Roberts said 'thank you very much' before scoring 42 per cent of all City's goals that season, which was more than Nottingham Forest scored collectively.

In 1925, at the age of fifty-one, City gave Billy Meredith a testimonial. For some reason. Meredith picked his own XI and somehow managed to get Rangers and Celtic to form the opposing side. 15,000 turned up to watch an old man trundle and toddle about, while everyone else played as though they were a three-year-old excited about the prospect of kicking a ball, only to fall flat on their arses when attempting to go anywhere near it. Bless.

The phrase 'Typical City' reared its ugly head, when, in 1926, they were the first team ever to reach the FA Cup Final (and scoring a staggering thirty-one goals to get there) only to lose 1-0 and be relegated in the same season.[4] This was just the first of many firsts that City would accomplish. Of course it didn't help that the club didn't actually have a manager at the time, resulting in each player giving themselves their own individual team talks, and what their role in matches would be, without actually informing anyone else of their decisions. One prime example was when the 'keeper James Mitchell had decided he would tell himself he would be better suited to play upfront and the team played for 27 minutes before realizing there was no one between the posts. 1926 also saw City defeat Manchester United 6-1 away, a truly amazing feat *never* to be repeated again.

In the 1926/27 season, City wanted to get back into the top-flight of football at the first time of asking, but fate conspired against them, and even a convincing 8-0 win versus Bradford City could not alter the course of events. Portsmouth were also in contention for that promotion spot, but their game had not finished by the time the whistle was blown at Maine Road. City fans celebrated only for Portsmouth to score in the closing seconds and win 5-1, meaning City missed out on promotion with a deficit of 0.5 per cent of a goal. This would be akin to playing in 'The world's best league' knowing you have won the title upon hearing the final whistle, only for another team to beat you to it by scoring twice in injury time and winning 3-2. City did win Division Two the following season though.

It was also during this 'roaring decade' that Manchester City's Albert Alexander, created 'The A-Team'; if Manchester City had a problem and if no one else could help, maybe they could ... simply run to this new group of young players, which was, in essence, an Academy (A-Team, you see?) and bring them into the first team. It was a clever move by Alexander, as these young fellas weren't being paid but were readily available to be used should the need arise, whether out of merit or necessity. Let's just hope the Alexander family are always in charge at the club, as I would hate to see what happens if someone else came in and forced them out.

The '30s finally arrived with the country knowing that England was heading for a wonderfully long peaceful period completely free from the threat of war. City, at this time, were not the most successful club in the country, but they were far and away the best supported and most well-known. And if this wasn't good enough, their red neighbours were not doing well at all, thank you very much for asking.

In fact, Manchester United were underperforming both on and off the pitch, and while they were a division higher than Manchester Central FC, they were pulling in much lower crowds than their Third Division neighbours; something had to be done.

Enter stage right, Manchester City to the rescue (again). The club, on behalf of Manchester United, petitioned the Football League in 1932, stating that Manchester Central FC was becoming a force majeure as far as the Reds were concerned and that they needed protecting from this minor insignificant lower league club. The Football League agreed and Manchester Central was kicked out, and immediately dissolved only to exist in the history books – much like this one. Everyone still blamed Manchester United though, so that was nice.

Now that City were fully established at Maine Road, tens of thousands of fans turned up every week.[5] The quality of football was getting better and better – well, maybe not straight away, they dropped to as low as sixteenth in the 1932/33 season, but ironically were runners-up in the FA Cup; a game that saw numbers being used on the backs of shirts for the very first time. City got lumped with Nos 12–22, meaning left-half Jimmy McMullan, got the No. 13 shirt (because they ran backwards – 'keeper Len Langford had the No. 22 for some reason), which effectively ruled him out as scoring or assisting a goal.

But there was a transfer in 1930 that made City fans collectively as a whole, stand up and say: 'You what mate, you did what now?' Tommy Johnson had been a sensation for the club after arriving from amateur side Dalton Casuals in 1918, regularly scoring goals and amassing a record breaking thirty-eight during the 1928/29 season; basically every time he kicked the ball with his left foot it was goalward-bound. He had cost the club nothing and in the days of paying players a mere pittance it had cost them nothing to keep him either. So when Division Two Everton, who were obviously ruining football, turned up with a bag of cash totalling £6,000, the fans presumed City would tell them where to stick their big bag of cash. And City did tell them where to stick their big bag of cash, by pointing to the club's bank account. The home support were mortified: 'He's past it,' they said, rather unconvincingly. 'We cash in now whilst we still can. Besides, Everton are in Division Two.'

Twelve months later, Johnson's goals had gotten Everton promoted and they were back in Division One. 'What?', said the City board. 'It's not like they are going to win Division One is it?'[6]

Anyway, proving that pushing for some silverware would not be detrimental to their league position, City did eventually get their second FA Cup trophy in 1934 (or was it their third?) during a massive thunderstorm at Wembley (and finished in fifth place in the League). After going into half-time one down due to a Frank Swift error in goal, Tilson, who had obviously been hanging around the gypsies, told him everything would be alright because he said he would score twice, which he then did. Why he didn't do this in every game is anyone's guess.

God Bless the *Manchester City*, and All Who Sail in Her, No. 2

How do you know how awesome you are? When you win the Division One title and have yet another ship named after you, that's how. So awesome was the *Manchester City* that the British Government decided to use her as a mine-layer during the Second World War, this time pissing off the Nazis instead of the Scousers.

That 1933/34 FA Cup campaign saw City attain the highest attendance ever recorded at an English stadium during a sixth-round match against Stoke on 3 March 1934 that ended 1-0. 84,569 *standing* people were there that day, although no one questioned how this was possible when Maine Road had a maximum capacity of just 80,000.

At the end of the 1936/37 season, City were crowned Champions of England for the very first time with club record signing Pete Doherty, netting 247 times. The fans celebrated by pointing ridiculing fingers at United, but the Reds were far too busy falling into Division Two to pay them any attention. What made this title-winning season all the more remarkable was that for the most part City played terribly (they usually did back then), with a run of one win in twelve and in the bottom half of the table in December. However, Santa turned up (albeit late because City lost on Christmas Day), kicked some bottom and the club went on a mental winning spree that culminated in them overtaking Arsenal in first place.

The club continued to celebrate in style by being the first English football team to play in the Berlin Olympic Stadium, after accepting an invitation of a playing tour of Germany from England's new best friend and all-round nice person, Adolf Hitler. Naturally, the etiquette of the day, dictated in a 'When in Rome' manner, that all should give the Nazi salute to our German overlords. The City players were none too happy about this and refused point blank, save for Frank Swift who decided to Nazi salute everyone at every conceivable opportunity – the German players, Germans in general, his own teammates, a cat, birds flying overhead, himself in the mirror, and faecal matter in the toilet. Sadly, City lost the match 3-2, but this was due, in part, to the German XI employing tactics mainly described as 'dirty cheating bastards'.

Unfortunately, something happened to the squad on that tour, because the following season they were relegated to Division Two, albeit by scoring more goals than any other team in the division.[7] Thankfully, however, that really nice chap, Mr Hitler, after hearing of the plight of Manchester City, said that some Polish person looked at him funny and proceeded to invade the whole of Europe, thereby giving City time to get their act together.

As was the case just prior to the First World War, City's financial department went into overdrive and bought a metric ton of players for a metric ton of cash, all of whom barely played – Albert Emptage, Eric Westwood, Les McDowell, Bert Sproston, Billy Walsh, and George Smith. Les McDowell cost the princely sum of £7,000, but only managed 118 games, but at least he came back after retirement to help win the FA Cup. Cheers, Les.

The League was abandoned for the second time in twenty-five years (with City officially finishing with just three points), and once again regional leagues took its place. Some City players continued to play for the club, others joined other teams and yet others took the easy option and went to war instead. Other than the first war league in 1940/41 and one in 1942, City were generally atrocious. Proving that no matter how bad the state the country was in, the club showed that things could be infinitely worse by finishing in forty-seventh place in 1945 with just nineteen games played. The season of 1942 saw City finish in an 'unplaced' position. At least they were knocking the goals in though.

A big admirer of City's 1880's shirt, Hitler ordered his Luftwaffe in 1941 to bomb Old Trafford instead of Maine Road, while systematically destroying the surrounding city, saying 'they are a crap club anyway – it's not like anyone will notice'. However, Manchester United did notice and were forced to come grovelling after the end of the Second World War to ask City if they could play at Maine Road. City remembered all the crap United had put them through a couple of decades earlier, but purely out of the kindness of their hearts not only did they say 'yes', but they also helped them out further by promoting United's fixtures and allowing them to have first refusal on all fixtures that clashed.[8] City did, however, refuse to allow United to use the home changing room during derby days, and neither were they offered the standard 20 per cent price reduction for the use of Wanda on Wednesday evenings.

United agreed to the terms laid down by Manchester City, which naturally included a yearly rental fee (of £5,000) and a percentage of matchday ticket sales. However, some City historians have suggested that this was never actually paid. The upshot of all this was that United, due to City simply wanting to help, grew bigger and more powerful (not possibly paying fees certainly helped) and actually started to get more support at home games than City did, even though it was the exact same stadium.[9]

It took City until midway through 1949 to remove United, mainly because half of the players chained themselves to the stands after every home game. It was a further eight years and five months before they got rid of the smell. But, as if that wasn't bad enough, Old Trafford was rebuilt using money through the War Damage Commission, meaning it was public money – City fans are part of the public, ergo, City fans paid for the rebuilding work.

1949 was also the year of the formation of the Official Manchester City Supporter's Club. For the first couple of years inclusion was only gained by fans after undergoing an initiation, which consisted of pledging their first unborn to the club and taking care of the club's pet cat on a rotating basis. Fans who refused were ridiculed by 'official' fans by way of them turning their backs towards them and jumping up and down (known as 'doing The Fagan').

One other thing of note after the war ended was for the club to change their strip. Although in what could only be described as 'cheap', they merely changed the name of the colour from 'light blue' to 'sky blue'. Shirts were still not yet sold to the public at this time, but one wonders if they would have fallen for it, had the club have done so.[10]

Happy Birthday Manchester City!
16 April

3-3 *v.* Burnley
1-1 *v.* Sheffield United
2-2 *v.* South Shields
0-0 *v.* Hull City
1-1 *v.* Chelsea
7-1 *v.* West Bromwich Albion
1-1 *v.* Sunderland
Good ol' West Brom; at least we are still undefeated on our birthday.

---

1 Okay, so maybe blaming the pre-war spending is a little harsh, but c'mon! Archduke Franz Ferdinand of Austria had just been assassinated and if that didn't set off alarm bells ringing on the City board of directors, then I really don't know what would.
2 More than likely the residual effects of the FA's 'fire and brimstone campaign' against the Blues.
3 Meaning City actually have the most Wembley appearances in history.
4 Awesome!
5 Sometimes even when there wasn't a game, because there really wasn't anything else to do in the 1930s.
6 Do I really have to explain what happened next?
7 Now that takes skill and dedication, the likes of which other teams could never understand.
8 Do you see what City did for your club, United fans? Do you? Oh, why do I bother.
9 This was due in part to many United fans being homeless with nowhere else to go.
10 Probably.

NOTABLE PLAYERS OF THE 1910S, 1920S, 1930S & 1940S

Andrew James Goodchild, 1911–27
If a scout in the employment of another club recommended an out-of-work goalkeeper to a different club in a higher league, because he hadn't been good enough to play in a lower league for the scout's club and been kicked out, do you think he would be snapped up and signed, becoming first-choice keeper? This is City we are talking about, so yes.

Albert Fairclough, 1913–19
Six years at the club. Five appearances. Hopeless. Utterly hopeless.

Billy 'Spud' Murphy, 1918–26
So called 'Spud' because Billy had an extra eye, this former English runner joined the club towards the end of the First World War (or 'the war' as they called it back then).

'Gentleman' Max Woosnam, 1919–25
This Cambridge-educated, fine, upstanding, handsome gentleman, who had won a Wimbledon title and a tennis Olympic gold, became City's first poster boy at the end of 1919. City's club shop didn't sell posters at the time (only leftover half-eaten meat pies from match days), so they sort of missed the boat on that one.

He joined the Blues from the amateur side Corinthians, a club that was the football equivalent of the Harlem Globetrotters because they constantly beat professional sides whenever they met, including defeating Manchester United 11-3, Blackburn Rovers 8-1, Bury 10-3, Derby County 6-0, and a cyborg XI sent back in time from the year 2107, 7-2. Manchester City, wanting some of this panache and style, brought this amateur defender into the squad.

Even though he was now a part of this working-class club, Woosnam refused to forget his status of 'one is so much more privileged than Northern scum', and so he was always seen playing with a silk handkerchief tucked in his tuxedo and a glass of Moët Chandon in his right hand. On several occasions, when he considered the pitch to be a 'tad rough', he would ask his chauffeur to drive him and the ball to the other end of the pitch, often resulting in several hit-and-runs.

Tommy Johnson, 1919–30

Tommy liked to win things and make extraordinary things happen. He was city's all-time leading goalscorer in one season with thirty-eight goals. He then went to Everton and helped them win Division Two, and then the following season, Division One. Off he trotted to Liverpool and saved them from relegation. Later, he was appointed as a UN ambassador and created peace and harmony throughout the entire world. However, he left this mortal Earth in 1973 upon hearing of Peter Swales' appointment – Tommy was good, but he wasn't that good.

Fred Gorringe, 1928

Gorringe holds the distinction of having the best goals to game ratio 2 to 1 at home. The fact that he only ever played one match for us is neither here nor there. *NB*: Yes, J. Dennilson in 1904 also accomplished this feat, but it was away to Blackburn Rovers so it doesn't count.

Fred Tilson, 1928–39

Fred, now in City's hall of fame, was a goal-hungry centre-forward with a strike rate of almost 1 in 2. He was also very breakable, and was often seen entering the field of play in a full-body cast.

Bill Dale, 1931–38

Most appearances by an outfield player (271) without scoring a single soddin' goal.

Frank Swift, 1933–49

Considered to be one of the best 'keepers ever to have played for City, however this may have been due to him possessing seven fingers on each hand and a hand-span of 45¼ inches. This also helped him type up articles in record-breaking time when he retired and became a reporter.

George Smith, 1938–51

Smith holds the unenviable distinction of signing for the club only for the Second World War to break out, meaning he didn't get a game for eight years. With nothing else to do he tended to the pitch, creating a wonderful cascading waterfall complete with wild lilies in the centre circle, which allowed him to sketch kingfishers. Word has it he was very pissed when the war came to an end and the groundsman demolished his work.

Giuseppi Luigi David Bacuzzi, 1941

'Cockney Dave' was a Fulham player, but he liked to spread himself about a bit, and the Second World War allowed him to do just that. After appearing for City in just one solitary game as 'guest of the week', he was threatened not to do so for Manchester United, but as City and United had not been in the same league before the outbreak of war, he decided appearing for them would not prove how big his balls were, which is why he played for Chelsea, and then a mere eight days later played for Arsenal. In your face, William Gallas.

Johnny Hart, 1945–61

Jo Hart, as they called him, had a strike rate of 1 in every 2.5 games. And how did City repay him? Peter Swales placed him in charge of the team for a few months in 1973. Pancreatic cancer, they said, forced him to step down. Yeah, I'd have said that, too.

Billy Spurdle, 1949–56

The country was still in tatters in 1949. Rationing was still in existence and the British had little hope for the future. Never mind, huh? City still had plenty of money, and proved it by splashing out £12,000 for Spurdle.

A Manchester City Fan of the 1940s Has His Say

Name: John Thomas
Age: 26
First City game ever attended: No idea, mate.

Why am I not in Europe? Dodgy leg, mate, an' me knees are gone, too. Y'see that twinge then? Ooh, ahh, real painful. I'd love to be there, but I can't see, I guess I'll just look after the women 'til their old fellas get back home.

Oh, City, yeah – well they ain't really playing, are they? Well, they are, but what's the point? Half the team has buggered off to war, an' they be desperate for some more players ... maybe I should give it a go?

Oh, hi, Doris, sweetheart. How's yer ma?

Oh, she's a bit of alright is that Doris – nice bit of skirt. Anyway, where was I? City. Right. Umm ... well, I think they got a game on tomorrow. Am I going? Dunno really, probably not. I've got that building guard duty thing tonight, lucky for me though it's at the Dog and Duck.

You haven't got any rashers of bacon, 'ave you? Cheer my mam up no end, would that. Chocolate? Lard? Stockings? Oh, never mind.

After the war? The way this things going, don't look like it's ever gonna end, does it? Me Mam says that someone should just do away with that Hitler fella, he's got no right running around and doing the things he does. But if it does end, then I guess we'll all make the most of it, 'cause us British are made of strong stuff, aren't we?

Hey, that's Joan over there, isn't it? Right gotta run, fella – God save the King!

I LOST MY HEART TO
A PARATROOPER

The war to end all wars had ended. The country was physically and economically in tatters due to six long years of fighting against the evil tyranny of the Nazis, with the outlook and prospects for all concerned being very bleak to say the least. But, hey, at least football was back!

This seemed as good a time as any for City to introduce their new goalkeeper, Bernhard Trautmann. To say that the local populace were not overly enthused about this new addition was akin to finding a tampon in your Lancashire hotpot.

Bernhard, or Bert once the City propaganda got into full swing, had been 'the enemy' during the war, only to be captured and taken as a British POW and now paraded around as the next best thing.

Women wailed, children cried, cats and dogs started doing it with each other, and Wanda stopped turning up on Wednesdays. However, Manchester City refused to pay any attention to this and, despite the threat of fans not turning up for the next game, the club threw Bert into the thick of things almost immediately. Of course, the threat was never actually carried out, or at least there was no noticeable reduction in the amount of hot cups of Bovril being sold on match days. This was due in part to City forcing the captain, Eric Westwood, to publicly welcome him to the club – Westwood had fought on the beaches of Normandy, doing his damnedest to blow Nazi brains out for more than half a decade. So if anyone could fool the press, it would be him. No one actually bothered to ask him what he really thought, which was just as well, considering the immense impact Trautmann was to have at the club.

The Manchester Jewish community, which had significantly multiplied during the war years with Jewish Europeans, gave their backing to Bert, stating that 'one man cannot be blamed for a Nation'.[1] Much to City's relief, Bert turned out not only to be a great 'keeper but an exceptional one, with his tendency to wander up the pitch and beat 10 tons of shit out of one of the opposition regarded by the club as a minor inconvenience.

'This is the age of the superstar,' said one City spokesman. 'When we get players who are taking drugs, assaulting our own players on the training ground, being imprisoned, refusing to enter the field during some European game, or having a pink bedroom in their own home, then we will consider it a problem.'

Bert was so good in fact that he made the rest of the squad look terrible. Actually, the rest of the squad weren't that good anyway and Bert just compounded the issue. Wilf Wild had wanted to bring in more players to balance the team's young (and not very good) and experienced (and not getting any younger) squad, but City told him they simply didn't have the money. For once this was true, after having to spend several thousand in making Maine Road safer after the Burnden Park tragedy of 1946. City were beginning to make a name for themselves that went somewhere along the lines of 'tight-fisted bastards', even to the point of refusing to reimburse Trautmann for a taxi ride to the ground, which he had to take due to train disruptions – I suppose City would have fined him if he hadn't taken the taxi then, yes? To be fair to the club, even though they only paid the players an extra £2 win bonus for the 1956 FA Cup, City asked the FA if they could give each player a gold watch as well. The FA promptly replied 'no, you can't', but it's probably just as well, as they more than likely would have fallen off the back of some lorry.

Gary says: 'Is he German? I hadn't actually noticed to be honest. Well, he was fighting the Russians, not the British, so he can't be all bad, now can he?'

The '50s were a strange decade for City, in that at times they played sublime football and in others they were positively diabolical.[2] City began the 1950s in Division Two (again), after being relegated in the 1949/50 season. The main reason for relegation was that City only managed to score thirty-six goals, with Liverpool FC their joint seventh highest scorer. They were obviously feeling sorry for City and tried to help by kicking the ball into their own net. That game still ended in a loss for the Blues and was part of a group of games where City didn't win once in thirteen games. There was a total of eighteen League games where City didn't even bother putting the ball into the back of the net at all.

At the end of the 1953/54 season, which had not gone particularly well (again), the German FA organised a five-match playing tour at the beginning of May, with City in West Germany in preparation for the 1954 World Cup in Switzerland. The request had been a simple one – come play five games against five West German teams and every time Trautmann featured Manchester City would receive £500. The only people who were happy about this was the City board of directors (obviously) and Trautmann himself, who was immensely proud of being able to play in front of his countrymen, something he had been unable to do thus far; the rest of the team could not be bothered one little bit. So it was no surprise when, in West Germany, the City players spent most of their time not in a game being in bars, and when they did actually play it was treated more like a kick-about than a true competitive match. Trautmann on the other hand was the exact opposite.

What was a surprise was that City never lost any of the West German Internationals – I suppose that would make Manchester City 1954 World Cup winners then.

Trautmann did injure his right leg in the penultimate game, but was forced to play once more (can't think why). That final 'friendly' game ended with Bill McAdams being sent off and the team ending up in a massive fight with the opposing team and some of the local Polizei. The large presence of stationed British Forces in the crowd were probably left unsure as to whether they should jump in or not, and, if they did, would that constitute as World War Three?

A couple of apologies and mutterings of 'you misunderstood that punch to the face' later, and City went back home, but without Trautmann. McDowall had instructed him to remain behind and seek out the very best treatment for his leg, which now had blood poisoning. 200DM (about £90 at the time) and two months later, Trautmann was fixed and he came back home to present City with his medical bills.[3]

In 1956 they did play brilliantly, culminating in winning the FA Cup by beating Birmingham City. Bert Trautmann finished the final 17 minutes of the game with a broken neck (after colliding with Birmingham's Peter Murphy) that should have killed him.[4] It had been a controversial road to Wembley because the fifth-round replay against Liverpool at Anfield should have ended in a draw and extra time, but the ref blew his whistle as Billy Liddel was about to shoot and the ref walked off as the ball went in. Nice one, ref. Then in the semi-final against Tottenham Hotspur, Trautmann decided that grabbing George Robb's leg and essentially 'clothes-lining' him would be a good idea. Apparently, so too did the ref, who didn't award a penalty to Spurs. Refs in the 1950s were awesome.

Additionally that FA Cup Final game was watched by a staggering 5 million people, and was the first match that the players were paid an appearance fee – a whole £5 each. As Birmingham were considered to be the favourites (who knows why), they managed to get the BBC to agree to sign them up to an exclusive contract featuring them several times in the run up to the game. However, Roy Paul was having none of this celebrity nonsense, calmly explaining this to his men and then showing them his clenched fist as they came out of the tunnel. Threatened with Violence FC 3 Celebrity Wannabes FC 1.

In the 1957/58 season, although finishing fifth after scoring 104 goals – more than any other team in the top two divisions – they also conceded 100 goals, which would have given them a mere +4 goal difference (not that the League used goal difference at that time, instead using a somewhat overly complicated goal average; football fans must have been exceptional at maths). However, the club were undoubtedly only starting to prepare themselves for the arrival of Kevin Keegan some forty-five years or so, later. This was followed by the 1958/59 season, which saw the team collapse to twentieth place, with what would have been a -31 goal difference. Trautmann was not best pleased. Mind you, after breaking his neck and only surviving because his third vertebrae didn't slip, he spent months on the sidelines and never quite hit the same level as he had done before. I suppose being told: 'Oh, it's just a crick, you'll be reet in t'morning; stop yer bloody moaning, have a whisky and go to bed,' will do that to a man.

Anyway, prior to this in 1953, a system was introduced to the reserve team that went by the name of the 'Don Revie Plan', which no doubt pissed off the Hungarians because he had stolen it from them after watching them outplay England at Wembley. It wasn't an instant success by any stretch of the imagination once this new style of play was brought into the first team, but eventually the players got the hang of it and it helped them to go all the way to Wembley and lose to Newcastle United in 1955.

In 1957, City attempted to recreate the success of the Revie Plan in the guise of the Marsden Plan, because Don Revie had been sold to Sunderland, in what could only be described as a good idea – or at least to someone in the City hierarchy. Up stepped Keith Marsden, who slotted into Revie's old position in City's seventh and eighth League games against Preston North End and West Bromwich Albion. 180 minutes and a combined scoreline of 3-15 later, Marsden never stepped out for City again.

In 1958, tragedy struck the Manchester United team when a plane crash occurred in Munich, instantly killing twenty people on board and twenty-three people in total.[5] Staggeringly, UEFA insisted that City take their place in the competition and told the FA to sort it out. However, City refused point-blank, saying it would have been disrespectful to their neighbours. For City's next game, virtually the entire match day programme was devoted to those who lost their lives and they even went to the extent of offering some of their own players to United to help them through it all. Trautmann offered his services to United as a translator to help them with communicating with the German authorities; United declined wondering why some Lancashire guy would know how to speak German. All of this is something that many, many modern-day United fans have completely forgotten about.[6]

Overall though, despite the tragedy in Germany, City were being outshone by their red neighbours throughout the decade, something that would begin to haunt them for a very long time (yes, we were that bad, that a team severely depleted in horrific circumstances were still better than us). City did manage to stay in Division One for the entire decade, after being promoted in 1951, although the following three seasons were very much touch-and-go, basically because they were, what we call, crap.

1953 saw Maine Road introduce floodlights after the FA had finally said they could be used for league matches (although it wasn't until 1956 that the first league game was played under them, which makes you wonder why we bothered installing them).[7] The first game at Maine Road using these night-time wonders was a friendly against the Scottish side Hearts, in which City wore special shirts that reflected the light. This resulted in several Hearts players to permanently lose their eyesight – oh, how we laughed.

This was actually not the first time City had played under floodlights, as the first time they had done so was way back in 1889 in a 'friendly' against Newton Heath, to raise funds for a recent Hyde Road mining disaster – coal miners were notoriously afraid of sunlight, so that was a nice touch.

But, sadly, it was not all good news, because the floodlights resulted in Manchester United returning to Maine Road to play various cup games for the next several years, due to the fact that they didn't have floodlights of their own because they couldn't afford them. And, no, I have no idea if they decided to pay us this time, or not.

Happy Birthday Manchester City!
16 April

1-0 *v.* Chelsea 0-1.
1-1 *v.* Charlton Athletic.
Still undefeated!

Notable Players of the 1950s

Dennis Westcott, 1950–52
A prolific goalscorer, Westcott scored a minimum of one goal every two games, no matter which club he played for, often becoming the top scorer of the season. For some reason, however, his clubs kept releasing him for free – perhaps he smelled a bit?

Johnny Williamson, 1950–55
Williamson was instrumental with the Don Revie plan playing as a deep-lying striker – so instrumental in fact that he barely played for the club, averaging less than ten games a season.

Roy Paul, 1950–57
Not content with spending a shedload of cash just before the Second World War, City paid Swansea Town almost £20,000 for this Welsh ex-miner (he's Welsh, what else did you think he used to do?). However, this time it worked out and Paul became invaluable to the side, not least as captain when he thought a player was not giving their all and he would beat the living crap out of them.

Don Revie, 1951–56
Named after the Hungarian style of play his mother was so fond of, this £25,000 centre-forward ... hang on, how much? Where's the club getting all this money from? I do hope this doesn't land them in financial difficulties later on down the road.

Colin Barlow, 1952–1963
Barlow joined the club as a schoolboy, only becoming professional in 1956, but carved out a fantastic career at the Blues and is currently still in the top twenty all-time goalscorers to this day. Neil Young ousted him out of the squad, so when he heard Franny Lee was taking over the club he decided to get in on the act by becoming City's first chief executive and help ruin it for everyone.

Billy McAdams, 1954–1960

Some people are described to have their lives etched into their faces; Billy's face was like a daily journal. Missing out on both FA Cup finals due to a severe back injury, Billy carved out a career creating 0.4 goals and 2.3 scars per game. His finest scar was caused when changing the radio station in his car, while driving ...

Bill Leivers, 1954–1964

Bill was part of the team that tried out the Revie Plan for the first time, only to come off injured and the game ending in a 5-0 loss. In a self-masochistic sort of fashion, Bill broke his nose over the course of his ten years at the club – one for every goal conceded that day.

Bobby Johnstone, 1955–59

Transferred from Hibernian for £22,000 ... oh, this is getting silly.

A Manchester City Fan of the 1950s Has Her Say

Name: Mrs Goodyear
Age: I don't believe that is very proper to be asking a lady of her age.
First City game ever attended: Oh, I don't go for that sort of nonsense!

My husband, now he does like his football. It's always the same with Bill, come in from the office, slippers on, favourite chair, turn on the wireless and see if he can find something nice. Of course, he does always turn to the sports pages in the newspaper, while I bring him a half glass of his favourite ale.

Oh, hang on, pet, I've got something in the oven ...

No, it's okay, the roast still has another good hour to go. So, what is this, some kind of survey? Are you from Her Majesty's Government? Manchester City won something you say? That's very nice, would you like a cup of tea?

Bill? Oh yes, he does go to that Maine Road stadium ground, not as much as he would like though. Me? Oh no, I don't understand it, I am much happier in the kitchen. Are you sure I can't make you something? It's no trouble you know.

Oh, look, here's Grace from next door, say hello to the nice man, Grace. I don't know, I think he's from the government – Grace's husband, Tom, works for the council, perhaps you know him. Tall fella, brown hair.

No, wait, don't leave, I've got some freshly baked scones, really nice with some homemade jam.

Oh, he's left … nice man, if not a little strange … anyway, Grace, you'll never believe what Angie said to me this morning…

---

1 Unless of course that 'one man' was called Hitler.
2 Something they would never repeat again. I said, NEVER!
3 You really don't think the club reimbursed him, do you?
4 The following year United's 'keeper Ray Wood would try and top this, but suffered a mere fractured jaw, and he went off too. Pussy.
5 No good ever comes from teams from the Greater Manchester area when they have anything to do with Germany. My advice is for everyone to stay well away.
6 And I am now reminding you.
7 Football floodlights had existed, in one form or another, since 1878, but I suppose that the FA saying 'yes' after seventy-five years of thinking about it is actually good going for them. Good on ya, fellas.

EVIL HAS A FACE AND IT IS ON THE CITY BOARD OF DIRECTORS

The 1960s were a pivotal period for the Blues, and just like it had been the case since pre-Second World War, they bounced up and down between Division One and Two like some nine-year-old on a concoction of caffeine and Ritalin. Towards the latter part of the decade, City did manage to accomplish one or two things that were described by some as being 'not too bad', but something occurred during the mid-1960s that needs highlighting. And it went by the name of Frank Johnson.[1]

Mr Johnson was at the time City's vice chairman, but always preferred to be called 'The Dark Lord' when being addressed by his secretary, Mavis. But what could this 'man' have done, that was so inexplicably evil? Was he a mass murderer? Was he after world domination? Did he single-handedly destroy the Earth's ozone layer resulting in everyone being scorched to death? No. What he attempted to do was far, far worse. He came up with the idea that Manchester City and Manchester United should merge and become one club.[2]

His evilness did not stop there though, because not only that (as if that hasn't made you go find your loved ones and seek their comfort in your time of need), but also decided that City's home ground would be Old Trafford, with Maine Road being immediately demolished. So adamant was The Dark Lord with his idea, that he kept it going from mid-1963 through the whole of 1964. Quite why he came up with it is anyone's guess, but he was determined to create Manchester Unity.[3]

City fans were naturally not best pleased with this news, and shareholders in the club led by a Peter Donoghue demanded that the entire board immediately resign, be stripped naked and forced to walk down Hyde Road pulling a No.168 bus with chains attached to their testicles.[4] Of course, the board eventually reconsidered their position, and listened to Donoghue's plan of action, which consisted of 'playing better, winning things, and beating Frank Johnson viciously every Wednesday evening'.

It was a good sound plan and it was one that was to pay off dividends in the late 1960s. Ironically, if it had not been for The Dark Lord's idea it is possible that the massive successes the club would have might never have happened, so, in that respect, does that mean Frank Johnson was a blessing in disguise?[5]

Gary says: 'Manchester City, Manchester United; there's no real difference, is there? Look, he just wants what is best for the club, and by club, I mean whatever the club ends up being called.'

The supporters had let it be known that this was their club and to this very day the fans are still considered to be the most important aspect of Manchester City. That is if you discount the untold wealth, the worldwide superstars who play for the club, the massive investment brought into East Manchester generating hundreds of jobs, and Mavis Goddard.

In 1960, when City were telling their players they had no money, which is why they had to use last season's holey socks and kits that were falling apart at the seams, they went on a mental spending spree, handing out a British record £55,000 for the one and only Denis Law. Manchester United had been after him, but somehow, even though United were finishing higher than City, we got him. It wasn't long before Law was quietly heard muttering: 'What the hell have I come here for? There's only the 'keeper and a couple of others who can actually play.' The outward appearance of the club was one of something immaculate and shiny, when the truth was the exact opposite. He lasted only one year. While Matt Busby would have loved to have taken him off City's hands, Italian side Torino slid in with a £110,000 cheque and off he went to southern Europe.

The players knew about the money City had received and, because of the FA removing the £20-a-week wage ceiling that year, they were eager to get their hands on some of it, especially considering that Fulham's Johnny Haynes was now on a 'millionaire's row' of £100 a week. One by one they trotted into the office, and one by one they trotted back out, not particularly pleased.

It got worse when Peter Dobing was brought in as a direct replacement for Law and was immediately offered £70 a week. Trautmann, who was already a legend for the 1956 Cup Final, had always been promised that 'we can't pay you more but trust us, if we could we definitely would,' was given a take-it-or-leave-it £30. Somehow, Trautmann eventually managed to get it to £35 (although he had to wait until the 1962/63 season for that), presumably after regaling them of Second World War horror stories. 'Vot you mean £30? Vell, I vill go to the foot of our RAF-bombed stairs!'

It didn't help matters that the players knew the club could pay them more, but refused to do so even though they now could. Other players from other clubs were getting a nice new pay packet, so why couldn't they?[6]

However, after Law left and before City got much better, they did in fact get much worse, so bad in fact that at the end of the 1964/65 season they finished in their worst position in their entire history – eleventh in Division Two.[7] During that season, Maine Road saw its lowest ever gates, sinking to as low as 8,015 against Swindon Town – which they lost. This was a very tough time to be a City fan.

God Bless the *Manchester City,* and All Who Sail in Her, No. 3

How do you know how awesome you are? By someone realising that your old namesake is getting on a bit and then building a brand new ship named after you, that's how. In 1971, South Korea bought the *Manchester City*, thereby pissing off the North Koreans with their awesomeness.

Fun Things To Do

Become 'tight-fisted bastard' City yourself by treating your partner to a delightful candlelight dinner for two at an expensive restaurant, then when the bill arrives leave them sat there alone while you run away with all the cash.

In 1965, the club introduced a new crest, replacing the Manchester coat of arms that had been used since 1894. It has to be noted that the lower half of the shield was red and gold, colours which were used by Manchester United during the 1950s; apparently Mr Johnson was still determined to bring his idea to fruition via the back door.

Also new in 1965 was the introduction of substitutions, after the FA realised that teams often going down to ten men wasn't the best situation. It didn't take City long to make use of this new rule, as in the fourth match of the season on 30 August, Mike Summerbee was replaced by Roy Cheetham. Still, had the rule been brought in in the 1950s Trautmann would have refused to leave the pitch.

The winter of 1967 saw what Kenneth Wolstenholme described as the most exciting team in the entire known universe when they went up against Tottenham Hotspur. At that time, hell had actually frozen over.[8] The UK was in the grip of weather so cold that at the very last minute on this day, Svetlana Alliluyeva, the daughter of Joseph Stalin, decided to seek political asylum with the United States instead of the UK, stating at the time, '*Мой картофель заморозится!*'[9]

Matches were being cancelled left, right and centre, but, after the referee – D. W. Smith – had inspected the pitch twice and declared he could see at least three blades of grass, the game was allowed to go ahead.

There were three things that happened that day, which guaranteed victory for Manchester City. One, Joe Mercer told his team that their family jewels were going to shrink anyway, so they might as well get used to the feeling, proceeding to send them all out on to the pitch one hour early. Two, discovering that there was no law against it, Mercer told his players to unscrew the studs from their boots, leaving only the small screws jutting out, adding that the Spurs player's skin would be so cold they wouldn't notice for hours if any of the City players were to accidentally attempt a 'surgical operation' on them. The third reason actually had nothing to do with City – the Spurs players wore white ... in the snow.

The media coined this game 'ballet on ice', when in actual fact it should have been called 'City sensibly prepare for wintry conditions, while Spurs wear white, in the snow.'[10]

In what was to become only the second time in the club's history, Manchester City did the un-typical City thing and actually won the top division that season, which led on to something that had never ever happened before, or indeed, since.[11]

It was that year (1968 if you've been keeping up), on 21 July, when Manchester City, as English champions, stepped out on to the pitch of Old Trafford to face European champions Manchester United – Old Trafford Cricket Ground, that is.

Between 12–15,000 football fans turned up that day (far more than most actual cricket matches managed) to watch what they thought would be an entertaining afternoon, which was actually a testimonial match for cricketer, Ken Higgs. It wasn't. Or at least it wasn't a sporting spectacle, as City, who went in to bat first, only managed 168 runs. What followed by the European champions was even worse – 79 all out. Manchester City were once again Champions, five kids got arrested for a minor pitch invasion that saw a police officer being assaulted and, for the first time since 1882, cricketers were shown once again by the Blues what it was to be manly.

After the fiasco that was Frank 'Dark Lord' Johnson (and suffering the indignity of their finishing position being the worst in eighty-five years), City brought in the aforementioned Joe Mercer who in turn brought in Malcolm Allison. This was the doing of Albert Alexander, who after seeing Mercer win the League Cup with Aston Villa, decided he was the man to bring City some silverware. The problem was that Mercer was quite happy at Villa and had no intention of leaving. One stroke and several complaints from Villa along the lines of 'What's with the face?' later, and Mercer was glad to be out and City glad to have him.

Mercer, who apparently understood what Alexander wanted, got City back into Division One immediately, with a tiny bit of help from new signings Mike Summerbee and Colin Bell. The following season saw Mercer showing how much he understood the typical City tag by guiding the team to the dizzying heights of fifteenth place. The rest of the League looked on in bewilderment at the talent on and off the field that City had, then shrugged their shoulders and wandered off. Of course this was all part of the grand Mercer/Allison plan, because City then won the League Championship, the FA Cup, the League Cup, the European Cup Winners Cup and a Blue Peter badge.

Trouble was, concerning the European Cup win, virtually no one saw the game against Górnick Zabrze ... some Polish side, because the Leeds *v.* Chelsea FA Cup Final had gone to a replay and the BBC had decided to screen that instead.[12] ITV, which was the only other television station at the time with the facilities to show it, didn't because they were in the midst of a 'colour strike' and 1970 Poland looked depressing enough as it was, and therefore showing it in black-and-white would have made it that much more worse.

The stadium – Prater Stadium – was a completely open arena, so that when it began to rain, the likes of which had not been witnessed since the days of Noah (or the previous week in central Manchester), it got so bad that there were actual reports of fans and members of the press drowning. A small section of the crowd did make the most of it with an inflatable dingy, only to get into trouble near the corner flag, causing the fourth official to call for the local lifeguard.

However, with goals (expert swimming) from Neil Young and Francis Lee (the former had practised 'water football' back in 1965 at Maine Road against Norwich City, scoring a goal in a match that was eventually abandoned due to flooding), it gave the Blues their much deserved win in Vienna and, when back in Manchester, thousands turned up to congratulate them/see if it wasn't all just a big wind-up.

In 1967, City brought forth the introduction of the Player of the Year awards, as voted for by the Official Supporters Club. The reason for this was all too plain to see – Manchester City were on the ascendancy, because, as already explained, one year later they were crowned champions and the following year won the FA Cup, the Charity Shield and the European Cup, and then the League Cup after that.

Now the club could parade their trophies and big name players who helped win these trophies; it was a winning formula and one that would continue for decades to come.[13]

Life for the supporters had never been so good, and they simply could not wait for the '70s to arrive in full swing.

Impress Your Pals in the Pub

Manchester City have never been beaten by the following five clubs in the League (where were you when they were shit?):
Colchester United
Macclesfield Town
Newport County
Scunthorpe United
Southend United

Happy Birthday Manchester City!
16 April

1-0 *v.* Spurs
0-2 *v.* Crystal Palace
4-1 *v.* Bolton
0-1 v. Chelsea
0-2 *v.* West Bromwich Albion

Excuse me, while I go and find Frank Johnson – there's someone in need of a right good kicking.

Notable Players of the 1960s

Denis Law (Part 1), 1960/61
Manchester United had done their best to get Law, so City threw £55,000 at Huddersfield to get him, which they did do. Two years

later United paid £115,000 to Torino to sign him. Yes, that makes complete sense to me as well.

Henry Dowd, 1961–70
Goalkeeper Dowd was kept out of the side by Trautmann, only to get the No. 1 jersey and lose it through injury to another 'keeper during the Championship-winning season. When he did finally get back in, he lost his place again to Joe Corrigan. He finally moved to Oldham Athletic where he reckoned all the 'keepers were utter shite.

Bobby Kennedy, 1961–69
Kennedy featured in eight seasons for the Blues, including the all-conquering 1967/68 season. They said he had not played enough games to warrant a medal, but it was more likely that he was the only non-English player at the club at the time – serves him right for being Scottish.

Mike Doyle, 1964–1978
City had had hard men before playing for them, but Doyle took it to an altogether different level. Rumoured to train the SAS during non-match days, Doyle was the sole reason for the Football League to introduce substitutions in 1965.

He was given a testimonial by the English National side on 9 May 1978, where, naturally, they allowed him to win, possibly in fear of being brutally beaten to death at full time.

George Heslop, 1965–1972
You might have thought that missing only one game in the 1967/68 season was a stand-out for Heslop, but you'd be wrong. He took over The City Gates pub, which was originally the Hyde Road Hotel, the pub where Ardwick became Manchester City. The author is a beer-drinking City fan, therefore Heslop is a legend.

Mike Summerbee, 1965–75
A most influential figure on the field, this City legend went on to star in *Escape to Victory*, with a supporting cast of Sylvester Stallone, Michael Caine and Max von Sydow.

Paul Hince, 1966–68
Two seasons and only seven appearances for City. That'll be why he wrote crap in the *Manchester Evening News* about the club all the time.

Tony Book, 1966–74
In terms of trophies, Book was, and still is, the greatest captain City have ever had – there was little the man could not do. He even survived the Peter Swales era!

Colin Bell, 1966–79
Greatest. Player. Ever. In the world. Ever.

Francis Lee, 1967–74
With a strike-rate of almost one in every two games (and most of those being penalties), plus ten goals against Manchester United, City with Franny could do no wrong.

Joe Corrigan, 1967–83
Standing at 8 feet 17 inches, this gentle giant was a reassurance to the City backline. Sadly, his international career had little chance of getting off the ground due to Ray Clemence and Peter Shilton. Bastards.

A Manchester City Fan of the 1960s Has His Say

Name: Mark Cressley
Age: 29
First City game ever attended: Oh, man, now you're asking me, things have been a bit fuzzy of late.

Yeah, they're doing really well, aren't they? Very crazy-train, and you know I can dig that. Yeah, I watch Match of the Day every now and then, but that's when I'm not getting with the groove. Hey! I've just had a wild idea! Julie is having a party at her pad tonight, you wanna come along? It's gonna be far out!

Hey, ain't no big thing, man, peace out, I understand you have to go along with your own groove.

Yeah, City, man, that Allison is far out. Very chilled. It's like he knows the score or something. And we got a black man playing for us! How wild is that?

Oh, sorry, man, didn't mean to wobble into you, I think it was those yellow ones I took this morning.

What were we talking about? Oh yeah, City. Very groovy. Hey! Julie is having a party tonight! Do you fancy coming along? I think she'd like you. Ok, no worries. I think I'll just hang here for a while and listen to some Dylan.

---

1 Evil, horrible, despicable! KILL! KILL! KILL!
2 Please see above.
3 An alternative would have been the anagram 'I C**t Deity' ... coincidence?
4 Read: Pitchforks and burning torches.
5 No.
6 Tight-fisted bastards! Were you not listening?
7 I reckon City could do worse than that.
8 Not to be confused with Wigan in late September.
9 No idea what that says – I don't speak Russian.
10 Seriously people. Am I the only one who can see a problem with this?
11 Calm down, calm down, it's okay – they'll soon get back to being crap again.
12 Bunch of 1960s bastards.
13 Hmm...

CONGRATULATIONS! YOU HAVE A COPY OF THE BOOK THAT HAS A BONUS CHAPTER!

(DON'T TELL EVERYONE, THEY'LL ALL WANT ONE)

Over the past eighty-five years, Manchester City had experienced a lot. But on 24 September 1965 – the club finally signed a non-white player.

Obviously the hoo-ha following the signing of a German paratrooper had died down and City knew they had to up the ante, so, Aston Villa's Stan Horne, who had previously played under Joe Mercer, was brought in and went straight into Mike Doyle's position at right-half.

In 'Typical City' fashion, his first appearance resulted in a solid performance and a home win, only for him to be injured during his second appearance and not play for another two months. This helped the City faithful accept Stan as one of their own – a brilliant move by all at the club concerned.

Stan happily stayed at the club for three years performing very well indeed, before moving on to Fulham FC, where he became – yup, you guessed it – their first non-white player.[1]

---

1 Throughout his life, Stan would only ever do things that non-white people hadn't done before, resulting in him being the first non-white to climb Everest, swim the Atlantic, land on the moon, and not be a very good dancer.

MANCHESTER CITY TAKES US ALL TO FUNKY TOWN

A Word From His Holiness Pontifex Maximus Pope John-Paul II

Hello? Is this thing on?

Beatus exsisto Manchester City, quod may omnipotens Senior nostrum Deus vultus secundum quod tutela lemma ex totus malum.

Blessed be the City fans for they are truly the chosen ones – God's own club. And you've now got the brilliance of Kazimierz Deyna, who has certainly been blessed with the gift from God almighty.

Sadly, he didn't want to grant me that particular gift when I used to play between the sticks in my youth, presumably thinking my talents would be better served elsewhere; who am I to argue? Still, one does wonder what could have been...

But, yes, Kazimierz – a wonderful, wonderful footballer, and now that you have him my blessings rain down upon thee; may God grant you all that your heart desires, and that He banishes your demons.

Swales? Well, God does work in mysterious ways, and we should not question Him, or doubt Him. He is omnipotent and omnipresent, the Alpha and Omega, the ... what? Well, okay, I suppose I could have a quiet word ... I have a direct line to Him, y'know.

But one must not wish harm upon others, we should have the patience and fortitude of our Lord, for it is written in the Scriptures that ... he did what? Surely you jest! But why? Why would he do such a thing?

Right, I must speak with the Vatican Council and the Sacred College of Cardinals at once. Hold steadfast, my child, may the Lord be with you.

Ah, the 1970s! When glamour, star-power and money appeared on the field, and beating 10 tons of shit out of each other appeared off it.[1] City were fined during the 1976/77 season because a fan physically attacked a Widzew Lodz player after he scored against them in a UEFA Cup tie. There was fencing at Maine Road at the time, but up until that incident there was nothing behind each goalline, which immediately changed after that game. What this did was to completely box in a large contingency of the home support, who were deemed to be a tad on the enthusiastic side,[2] but the fencing only seemed to exacerbate the problem, which continued for almost two decades.

But why were we in the UEFA Cup? Because in the 1975/76 season we had won the League Cup, which was the first thing City had won since hoisting the UEFA Cup in 1970. City had re-found their mojo, and it was obvious to all that there would be many, many, many more trophies coming their way in the next few years.[3]

It is important to note that City and their red neighbours were not the worst for hooliganism, but because of who they were everything was blown out of proportion, resulting in the FA clamping down hard. United were actually worse, but this was due in part because they held the honourable distinction of being the first ever club to win in a European competition and be relegated, which was somewhat amusing.[4]

The rivalry on the pitch between the Manchesters and Traffords of this world really began to pick up pace during this decade. Before, while competitive games were generally good-natured affairs, they were not so in the 1970s. The reasoning for this was likely to be a case of United winning the top title in the 1950s three times, and twice in the 1960s, which as it turns out should also have been three times (well, according to them anyway), but City beat them to it. Suddenly everything changed – United were pissed – and on derby days fans would be lucky if they saw a football match break out.

Gary says: 'Boys will be boys. Football offers a release to these men, and clinical studies prove that one needs an outlet – the three-day working week can only keep men busy for so long.'

In 1970, George Best attempted to surgically remove Glyn Pardoe's leg, the following season Francis Lee was throwing himself on to the pitch every time the ref looked at him in a 'look at me, look at me!' manner, and in the 1973/74 season both Mike Doyle and Lou Macari got sent off but refused to leave the pitch, leaving the ref to grab the ball and tell everyone it was his and that he was going home. We won't mention 1975, lest I break down and cry.

United also saw City (seemingly, but, as we will learn, not actually) on the ascendancy, while they had just lost a brilliant manager with Bobby Charlton having all but retired and Bill Foulkes having done so, and their rather temperamental Irishman becoming more and more temperamental by the day.

At the beginning of the 1972/73 season, the Charity Shield, as it was then known, was won by Manchester City after beating Aston Villa (at Villa Park no less) 1-0 by virtue of yet another Franny Lee penalty. Thing was though, that City had won neither the League or the FA Cup the previous season, and were there only because the FA had asked them to play. This was true of Aston Villa, too, but at least they had just won Division Three. Derby County (league winners) and Leeds United (FA Cup winners and League runners-up), who were to play, told the FA 'no thanks', which should have led to third place Liverpool being asked to play. Liverpool did go on to win the League title and the UEFA Cup later that season, so this could have been a very nice treble (of sorts) for them. Ah, well, never mind, huh? Cheers, fellas.

A few months earlier, in March 1972, Manchester City, or to be more correct, the Manchester City squad, did something that is ranked as one of the best things ever done in the history of mankind – they recorded 'The Boys In Blue', which was produced by none other than Godley and Creme. It came along with the equally awesome B-side 'Funky City' in giant, flared pants, aeroplane-collared shirts and where-do-the-sideburns-end-and-the-beard-begin manner, which consisted of no lyrics save for those in the title, meaning even the most inebriated could sing along with Godley and Creme. This musical masterpiece was released as a 7-inch single on 14 April by RCA, leaving fans wondering if there was nothing that Colin Bell couldn't do.[5]

Sadly, the record was only sold in and around Maine Road, and while it obviously sold in the billions, none of them were registered as a 'chart sale' – if they had done, it would still be the current No.1 to this very day – but this was due to the evilness that was Chelsea FC. They had just released the 7-inch single 'Blue Is The Colour', a couple of weeks earlier, which, while the title was factually correct, referred to the wrong shade of blue and they knew it, too. A quiet word in a few people's ears later, and they entered the Top 40 as high as fifth place, whereas City was nowhere to be found.

However, something far more catastrophic happened at the club and for that we must head on into 1973, when a man walked into the club and took it over. Peter Swales was a successful Manchester business man and a huge City fan, and while that sounded like a winning combination, it wasn't long before fans were wondering whether Frank Johnson hadn't been that bad.[6]

He came to the club with just one vision – be bigger than Manchester United. Had anyone pulled this self-proclaimed City fan to one side and explained what City had accomplished during the last five years, and what United had accomplished in that period, he may well have said 'Oh, yeah. Well, never mind then, I guess I'll go home.' Sadly, nobody did, so he stayed. For twenty long years he stayed. Twenty![7] Swales had in fact been at the club in one form or another for the two years prior to this, but then seized control from the excellent 'Yes, we're doing a damn fine job, and don't need anyone to screw it up now,' Alexander family.

His position, however, was watertight[8] due to the unwavering support and backing of Stephen Boler and Greenhalls Brewery, both of which were major shareholders (with the latter being the seventy-fourth brewery in charge of the club).

Swales also brought in a new crest for the club, and quite lovely it was, too, featuring a ship sailing merrily along, above the symbol of Lancashire: a red rose. The following year, on 1 April 1974,[9] Manchester was literally 'moved' out of Lancashire and firmly placed into the new metropolitan county of Greater Manchester. It wasn't like Swales was not aware of this, as the Local Government Act of 1972 was set up for this very purpose. Still, at least Manchester United could finally say they actually were now in Manchester (sort of).

At the time of Swales' arrival as the 'main man', Malcolm Allison was at the helm, after Mercer had been forced out – not least by Allison himself. The reason for this was because when Swales was attempting a takeover, he had promised Allison the manager's position. Mercer, on the other-hand, was an Alexander man. Sadly the brilliant and successful lost to the inept and deluded.

However, for Allison, repeating the immense successes, or any for that matter, was out of reach, and the fans were starting to turn on their new manager; so Allison resigned. That plan went well, didn't it, Mr Swales? Let's see what you do next...

In came ex-City player, Johnny Hart, but he lasted about six months before being forced to leave due to ill health, so Tony Book, who at the time was still playing for the club, was given the nod by Swales until a suitable replacement could be found for Hart. The suitable replacement Swales found was Ron Saunders, but the trouble was that he wasn't actually suitable, or at least the 'suitable' that Swales wanted: 'You can't get me excited by taking us to the League Cup Final and then losing to bloody Wolves!'

Swales once again turned to Tony Book, who promptly hung up his playing boots for good. Considering Swales' hatred for Manchester United – which bordered on the unhealthy – Book's first season in charge that saw the infamous Dennis Law back-heel derby victory at the end of the 1973/74 season, resulting in the relegation of the Reds, must have given Swales a full-on chubby for the fella.

His heart probably did stop for a second or two when the United fans tried and succeeded in getting the game abandoned before the ref had blown for the final whistle by way of a mass pitch invasion. But after a review, the Football League decided that the result would stand and that no replay was necessary. Sadly, Law was immediately substituted from that match and never played a League game again, but Swales rejoiced (not about the Law thing, but about the law thing).

Then, in 1976, Book brought the League Cup to Maine Road and, in 1977, City finished just shy of Liverpool in second place by one solitary point – finally Swales had found the right man to bring City back to its glory days.

Well, at least that is what the fans thought, but we are talking Swales here, and we are forgetting his main objective. A cup was all very well, but the question was always, 'Did we finish above United?' 'Yes,' had always been the answer. That was until the end of 1979, when the answer became an emphatic, 'No.'

That one solitary word was enough for Swales to remove Tony Book and replace him with Malcolm Allison again. Great things were expected of Allison and indeed great things were delivered, or at least they were if you consider spending vast amounts of money on poor players and removing all the good ones as delivering great things. Remember Steve '£1,437,500' Daley? He didn't just break City's transfer fee, but broke the British record transfer fee, too. Biggest waste of money in footballing history was how I recall the *Observer* describing it in 2001. I would have thought paying to watch City play in the 1980s was a bigger waste of money.[10]

However, Allison later revealed that he had initially agreed a fee with Wolverhampton Wanderers for Daley, of three chocolate biscuits and an evening with their rather attractive club secretary, Stacy; that was until Swales stepped in.

'We'll show United who's got the money!', he cried aloud, clasping his hands together while bending forward slightly and rotating his behind. A year earlier, however, Swales had not 'shown the money', but in fact had 'shown the Staples', when the club signed Polish midfielder Kaziu Deyna, who was at the time essentially in the army. Quite why the Polish military wanted to arm themselves with fax machines is anyone's guess. Exocet missiles? No thanks, we've got ourselves a rather nice switchboard.

Pop Quiz – Hotshot

Which was worse?
A: Living through two world wars?
B: Surviving the Great Depression?
C: Being born in Old Trafford?
D: Witnessing what Peter Swales was doing to our great club?
If you chose 'D', then congratulations, you're L. S. Lowry. Unfortunately, 'D' was so much worse than the other three he had been forced to endure, that Lowry couldn't take it any more and passed away.

Do you see what you are doing, Swales? Hey! Don't ignore me, I'm talking to you ...

Forty-one years after making their debut in the 1934 FA Cup final, Umbro became City's official kit supplier – no longer would it be the responsibility of the cheapest tailor that could be found on Manchester Road in Manchester, but of a world-renowned sports clothes manufacturer on Manchester Road in Wilmslow. They had supplied the British Olympics team, almost every international football team, and virtually every professional domestic football side in the UK, so when they finally got around to supplying Manchester City we obviously became their crowning jewel. Obviously.

Reference was made at the beginning of this chapter to the beginning of the age of the superstar in the footballing world, so what better way to remember and honour the superstars of the past than to rename eleven streets in one of the worst areas of Manchester after eleven City players? That'll sort out all the problems that Moss Side was facing.

However, come the mid-2000s, those eleven streets (Sam Cookson, Frank Swift, Fred Tilson, Sam Cowan, Horace Barnes, Max Woosnam, Tommy Browell, Jimmy McMullan, Eric Brook, Billy Meredith, and Tommy Johnson)[11] had dwindled down to just four, with five of them becoming 'walks' or footpaths,[12] and two – Frank Swift Street and Max Woosnam Street – completely vanished.

Manchester ~~United~~ Council had decided that 'The closures were implemented to permit redevelopment of the sites to take place', which as we all know means, 'It's like when you go to the grocery store and the night staff have changed everything around, so milk is no longer on aisle four, and you have to go looking for it, but now you think everything is new and shiny, when in actual fact we haven't done a damn thing, or spent any money, we've just made it more confusing.'

And so the 1970s came to a close. What had started out as a decade of promise and being winners had ended in fiasco and very little to show for it, save for managing for the first time in our history to remain in the top flight for an entire decade. Swales had allowed Allison to walk into the changing rooms with an assault rifle and rip the heart of the team apart, so why he was shocked when we finished seventeenth, with Michael Robinson, the club's highest scorer, not even reaching double figures, is anyone's guess. Swales had created the mess, and he was the only one the fans could look to to rectify it.[13] He vowed never to allow the systematic dismantling of the side again and promised that City would not only keep their players but add strength to the side. So surely the 1980s would be the decade to bring back the glory?

Happy Birthday Manchester City!
16 April

0-4 *v*. Liverpool.
2-0 *v*. West Bromwich Albion.
At least the Brummies know whose birthday it is.

Notable Players of the 1970s

Colin Bell, 1966–79
Did I mention he is the greatest player in the world? Ever? 1979 was a very bad year.

Rodney Marsh, 1971–75
Phenomenal ball-holding skills saw Marsh bring something extra to City's game. Sadly, City preferred to keep the ball moving in a free-flowing style.

Denis Law (Part Two), 1973–74

Law, who had been at United since 1962, had suggested to the board that Tommy Docherty, someone he knew quite well from his international career, should become the new manager. The board agreed and appointed him, only for Docherty to transfer Law out of the club. After a total of £280,000 worth of transfers, Law ended up back at City on a free. Unfortunately, for this footballing legend, things didn't quite go according to plan.

The Circle of Law

Law begins career at Huddersfield – United want Law – Law goes to City for a British record fee – United want Law – Law goes to Torino – United eventually get Law for a British record transfer fee – Law gets Docherty appointed – Docherty gives Law away for free – Law plays for City and relegates United – Docherty gets fired for doing the dirty.

Asa Hartford, 1974–79 and 1981–84

Asa was to move to high-flying Leeds United until it was discovered that he had a hole in his heart. City misunderstood this and promptly signed him, after Swales was heard asking 'A hole? But everyone's got one – how else would they go to the toilet?'

Gary Owen, 1975–79

A City lad through-and-through, Gary cost the club absolutely nothing as he joined at the age of fourteen. He became an integral member of the team's midfield, and was adored by the home crowd. That'll explain why Allison sold him then.

Paul Power, 1975–86

Awesome name, and fantastic 1970s porno 'tasche. Twelve years this Mancunian played for City, but he had to move to Everton to get his hands on a major trophy. Mind you, at least he got away from all the 'boo-boys'.

Steve Kinsey, 1979–86

Kinsey did a relatively good job for City, scoring an average of a goal every seven matches, but it was what he did after he left the club that made him stand out. Seventeen different clubs and four different countries in just eleven years. Eat your heart out Nicolas Anelka.

A Manchester City Fan of the 1970s Has His Say

Name: Steve Wendle
Age: 34
First City game ever attended: 1969 FA Cup Final, with me Dad.

C'mon you Blues! C'MON!!! We can beat the dirty Reds! And crack some skulls while we are at it. Huh? Why? 'Cause they are red, that's why, they're nothing but bastards.

No, mate, you don't understand – you saw what they did to Colin Bell! Well, yeah, I know it wasn't their fault, but what are you gonna do? … Do I know what? We used to get on? We did? Walking side by side, you say? That's not gonna happen now, is it? Tommy got a good kicking last week … by United fans? No mate, but they don't know that, do they?

Why are you shaking your head, pal? You don't understand … it's just that … umm … well … Susan left me last week. I miss her so much. Can I have a hug? Umm … no, just got something in my eye, that's all.

Actually, the Reds – they're alright really, I mean it's not their fault they can't support a proper club, is it? Mind you, with what that Swales is doing to our club is an absolute joke. Who does he think he is? Well, he knows who he is, but it ain't what we reckon he is.

Oh, Susan, why did you leave me? I know you are a Red, but we could have worked it out…

The English Have Always Enjoyed a Good War, Trouble Is if City Are to Benefit, They Need to Choose More Carefully in Future

WHO? Burma
WHEN? 1885
CITY'S PERFORMANCE DURING THE WAR? Iffy. Lost one, drew one, but then won 4-1 the day after the war ended.
FUTURE WAR? Unlikely, but if it does happen, get your arse down to the bookies and place everything on a big win for City.

WHO? China
WHEN? 1899–1901
CITY'S PERFORMANCE DURING THE WAR? Promising, but then ended in disaster when we were relegated.
FUTURE WAR? You never know. Do you miss playing away to Macclesfield?

WHO? South Africa
WHEN? 1899–1902
CITY'S PERFORMANCE DURING THE WAR? Same as China.
FUTURE WAR? Highly unlikely, so maybe we'll be going to war with Millwall instead.

WHO? Germany, Austria-Hungary, Ottoman, Bulgaria
WHEN? 1914–19
CITY'S PERFORMANCE DURING THE WAR? Bloody brilliant! First place three times!
FUTURE WAR? Bring it on.

WHO? Ireland
WHEN? 1919–21
CITY'S PERFORMANCE DURING THE WAR? Not too bad, only for peace to break out and City tumbled down the League.
FUTURE WAR? Note to self: keep hold of the potatoes.

WHO? The Evil Axis
WHEN? 1939–45
CITY'S PERFORMANCE DURING THE WAR? You want goals? You want lots of goals? Jim Currier scored fourty-seven in one season alone!
FUTURE WAR? Titles and Golden Boots? Yes, please!

WHO? North Korea
WHEN? 1951–53
CITY'S PERFORMANCE DURING THE WAR? City had just been relegated only to see consolidation and promotion during it.
FUTURE WAR? They are batshit mental, so who knows? Best keep 'em hanging around in case China goes crazy.

WHO? Kenya
WHEN? 1952–60
CITY'S PERFORMANCE DURING THE WAR? So-so, but we did get an FA Cup out of it.
FUTURE WAR? Yo-yo'ing up and down the League for most of the decade and only one trophy to show for it: Nah, not worth it.

WHO? Egypt
WHEN? 1956
CITY'S PERFORMANCE DURING THE WAR? We won the FA Cup!
FUTURE WAR? Not won anything in ages? Egypt is your man, although we have paramedics on stand-by if there are any Germans in the squad.

WHO? Argentina
WHEN? 1982
CITY'S PERFORMANCE DURING THE WAR? Not great. Dropped from first place to tenth virtually overnight.
FUTURE WAR? Falklands or titles? Just asking.

WHO? Gulf War – Iraq
WHEN? 1990–91
CITY'S PERFORMANCE DURING THE WAR? Respectable. We finished fifth.

FUTURE WAR? Oh, it's coming, don't you worry.

WHO? Desert Fox – Iraq
WHEN? 1998
CITY'S PERFORMANCE DURING THE WAR? No! No! No! No!
FUTURE WAR? Once you go Muslim you never go back.

WHO? Yugoslavia and Serbia
WHEN? 1998–99
CITY'S PERFORMANCE DURING THE WAR? Aaaaaaaarrrrgh!
FUTURE WAR? Praise be unto God that Yugoslavia doesn't exist anymore.

WHO? Afghanistan
WHEN? 2001 and still going!
CITY'S PERFORMANCE DURING THE WAR? Started out not so great … but then we became frickin' awesome!
FUTURE WAR? Reckon we need to finish this one first, hey?

WHO? Iraq … again
WHEN? 2003–11
CITY'S PERFORMANCE DURING THE WAR? We'll teach 'em not to screw around with God's own club.
FUTURE WAR? Job done, let 'em be.

---

1 Sweet memories.
2 Read: Mental.
3 Well, when I say 'obvious', what I really mean is 'not at all obvious'.
4 Still is, actually.
5 No, there isn't.
6 If that doesn't explain it enough for you, then take a look at the Facebook page set up for Peter Swales. It has only one 'Like'.
7 TWENTY!
8 Arse and duck springs to mind.
9 Insert your own joke here.
10 You can use that one on one of your dinner speeches, Steve.
11 There'd have been a Roy Paul street, but people would have been too scared to live on it.
12 A 'walk' in Moss Side is basically an on-foot escape route from the chasing police.
13 There may be trouble ahead...

MANCHESTER CITY LOVES THE 1980S

A Word from Former President of the United States – Abraham Lincoln

I've always had a bit of a soft spot for Manchester, after all, the working men of the city suffered greatly in miserable abject poverty due to us trying to stop slavery – sorry about that. Mind you, as a result, most of Tameside sailed off to Australia and New Zealand permanently, so silver lining and all that.

Anyway, we won, in case you had been wondering, not that I got any thanks for it. I used to be on the $100 bill, then I got demoted and now it's just the $5 and that damned penny. But you like me, right? You even have that nice bronze statue of me in the square, which is named after me, too. That's touching, that is.

But I am not here to talk about me, I am here to talk about Manchester City; after all why do you think I made my soldiers wear blue when fighting against the umm … also blue uniformed Confederates. They did eventually start wearing grey though … however, I recall an old Dutch farmer, who remarked to a companion once 'that it was not best to swap horses when crossing streams.' Sensible man, I must say, well for a Dutch farmer, at least.

But there's the thing, you see, Manchester City seemed to have done nothing of late but cross streams. And what else have they done? Anyone? Hello? Is anyone actually listening?

Horses! No, managers. Well, it is the same thing. Swapped so often, the club keeps drowning. Ne'er will you get to the other side, oh no, Sir, you will not. And I once stated, 'A house divided against itself cannot stand,' which I believe is also appropriate. I seem to recall I also said something about America and freedoms, but I am not sure that that applies in this case.

But, yes! City could do worse than heed my words. Huh? Swales? Sounds like the damned Confederacy, if you ask me. Does he keep slaves? I am not sure that Tony Book counts, but I think he should get out while he still can.

I did say, a long time ago, that 'the best way to destroy an enemy is to make him a friend' – obviously I wasn't talking about Peter Swales. Advice? Not sure, really. Have faith that someone will ride in and rescue you all from his vice-like grip; I'm sure it will happen very soon.

After the nightmare of Swales' decision to bring back Allison, what followed was City's much heralded 'revolving-door policy', and very successful it was too, with no less than eight different managers during the 1980s. Awesome stuff. Quite incredibly, Tony Book was reinstated as No. 1 for one game, while Swales got John Bond in through the door. This was after City had failed to win any of their first ten League games under Allison, although he had steered City to the third round of the League Cup, which as we know accounts for nothing.

What was to be an interview for the position of a new manager was made all too clear that it actually wasn't, deduced by Swales' manner of 'I don't care what the board thinks, I made my mind up last week, so I'm just going to sit here and fiddle with my … ooh! Cookies!'

City spent this decade doing something else they had previously proved to be exceptionally good at: relegation and promotion. However, it wasn't all doom and gloom, because they played in the FA Cup final against Tottenham in 1981 and … lost. This was due, in part, to City's Tommy Hutchison scoring twice – unfortunately.

There were some brighter moments like beating Huddersfield Town 10-1, and of course beating the Heathens 5-1 (which wasn't as big a deal as it looks because United were just about as crap as we were back then), but to be quite honest these wins were very few and

far between. What the fans really needed was something to be proud
of once more, something that they could really throw themselves
into.[1] Step forward, Frank Newton.

Frank was essentially a nobody, other than being a City fan, and a
light-hearted kind of guy, but what he did on 15 August 1987 changed
City and football forever.[2] During the game against Plymouth Argyle,
Frank started waving an inflatable banana about, dressed in his City
shirt. Many an observer ridiculed Frank, but he was unrepentant.
As the season wore on, Frank's banana was seen at every game and
oh how we laughed. But it needed just one more ingredient – enter
stage-right, Imre Viradi.

During the West Brom game in November of that year the fans
were calling for the appearance of Viradi, but somehow for some
reason the fans started calling him Imre Banana, and at that moment
the perfect storm was formed.[3]

It did get to a point where at some games the bananas seemed to
outnumber the fans, causing the City hierarchy to consider charging the
bananas full admission price. Of course some supporters attempted to
bring their own brand of humour by introducing different inflatables
like sharks, penguins, beer bottles and, as seen during a Bradford game
in 1989, an 8-foot-tall bouncy castle, complete with ball pit.

It is interesting to note that Arsenal FC banned the bringing of
inflatable bananas to their games. It obviously didn't stop Arsenal
fans taking the real thing to other games, as was evident when
Adebayor was deemed to be low in potassium in 2009.

1982 saw City join a long list of other teams who now proudly
received a big bag of money by way of wearing the name of a
sponsor on their shirts. Liverpool had been the first to do this in 1979
using the global electrical giant, Hitachi. Derby County would have
claimed to be first, but, upon hearing that Saab had sponsored them
in 1978, the Football League refused to give permission to the club to
wear the name of the car company on their shirts, even though Saab
had paid up front and given every County player a new car for free.
'A free car?' said Swales, 'that'll do nicely.'

However, the free cars were only for a very small number of board
members – not that Swales minded – and the players never even got

a sniff of that new Swedish car smell because to have done so the sponsor contract said they had to win the League. Not only that, but Swales gave the reputed £400,000 for the two-year deal straight to the bank manager. What was that about you wanting to do better by strengthening the side, Swales.

So were the 1980s all about relegation and promotion, and managers who were told there was no point having their name on the office door? In a word, yes. Of the 422 League games played, City managed a 36.9 per cent win ratio. To put that into some sort of perspective, it was the lowest win percentage of a single decade that City has ever managed – they even played better than this during both world wars.[4] To cap it all off, the Football League had introduced three points for a win from the 1981/82 season, because it would encourage more attacking football; evidently, Manchester City had not received this memo. All football clubs go through bad patches at one time or another, so in that respect we will simply call the 1980s 'a patch'.

Yes, the patch was bad. While the world rejoiced with awful hairstyles and danced to synthesized pop, City were doing their utmost to create a mirror image of the 1960s, only realizing too late that anything seen in the mirror is reversed and therefore the exact opposite.

Many of the problems were attributed to the board of directors, who at times seemed to act like the insane bad guys from a 007 movie. Ironically, as already mentioned, they brought in John Bond to replace Allison, who actually did a respectable job in the face of such insanity. The original Crazy Gang watched Bond, John Bond, bring City back up from seventeenth during Allison's reign, to twelfth and then tenth. It is hard to know if he was then fired or resigned, but because we are talking Crazy Gang/arch-villains, we'll go with the former.

RULE 34
If something bad has ever happened at a football club, it has also happened at Manchester City.

RULE 35
If something bad has yet to happen at Manchester City, no doubt they're working on it.

This was the point in time when things started to go from bad to worse. In the 1982/83 season, City were at the top of Division One a little before Christmas. One sacking and five months later, City were fourth from bottom and perilously close to being relegated before entering the final game against Luton Town (who were third from bottom), needing anything but a loss to stay up. Ironically, Luton needed a win to stay up, normally an infinitely more difficult thing to do away from home, unless of course you are playing against City who cannot afford to lose. Which of course they did … by one goal – a deflected goal scored with 7 minutes left on the clock. At least David Pleat appeared to be happy.

John Bond's right-hand man, John Benson, who came with him from Burnley, had taken over managing the club, and by the end of the season had become City's worst ever manager, with a 17.65 per cent win ratio.

It was also this season when the home support (and a lot of away support, because it was seen as the fashionable thing to do) began to turn on their chairman. It had been bubbling under the surface for quite some time, but the wigged-wonder suddenly got it in the neck as City once more descended into Division Two; 'Swales out!' had a nice ring to it.

If the truth be known, Swales wasn't bothered what the fans thought; megalomania can do that to a person. He was much like a gambler at the roulette table who keeps betting to get his money back from all the previous losing bets. Unfortunately, Swales kept putting all his money on zero.

Anyway, Swales, not believing that the Scottish John Benson spoke for all of Scotland, turned to Billie McNeill to quickly take the club back up to Division One; McNeill was supposed to be going to take charge of Manchester United, so one can only imagine Swales' thinking behind getting his man: 'We can still beat United even if we are in a different league.' If the truth be known though, United wanted Ron Atkinson, as the club would never ever employ a Scotsman to manage their team again.[5]

Live Life as Peter Swales

Go visit your Aunt; choose the best chair; sit down and refuse to ever leave, explaining that you know what's best for her, and that what is actually best for her is to spend all her money. Oh, and get her a new husband every five months.

McNeill almost managed it, too, getting the club to fourth by the end of his first season. Trouble was, fourth place was ten points behind third, with almost twice the better goal difference. The following season became squeaky-bum time, as it was only a superior goal difference of five more than Portsmouth that saw City promoted instead of them – in your face 1927, you ain't laughing now are ya, Pompey?[6]

Now, Swales could get back to asking his favourite question, and with Ian Brightwell, Steve Redmond and David White moving up from the youth team, he expected that answering that question would be easier.

Quite amazingly, at the end of the 1985/86 season, even though the answer to the question was 'no', McNeill stayed on for about a month and then buggered off to Aston Villa. McNeill explained that having no money to spend was his primary reason for leaving the post; that and the fact he didn't get on with the new director Freddie Pye, who was known for his absolute bluntness – 'Do I look fat in this?' 'Yes, and you look positively hideous, as well.'

God Bless the *Manchester City,* and All Who Sail in Her, No. 4

How do you know how awesome you are? By someone realising that the ship they have isn't awesome enough and then it is renamed after you, that's how. In your face, *City of Lisbon* ship.

However, the *Manchester City* is now in the hands of the Malaysians, and, yes, it is no longer called the *Manchester City.* The bastards.

Let them have their stupid ship, with their stupid name of *Mild Victory.* Mild Victory? Relative Success? Minor Win? We Did Okay But Not Really? Perhaps We Shouldn't Have Bothered? Meh?

Mind you, there's never been a ship called the Manchester United, which is somewhat surprising considering who bought this ship ...

Once again, Swales, believing that there existed a managerial footballing genius in Scotland, brought in Jimmy Frizzell, who expertly guided us to twenty-first place and a return to Division Two along with massive debts. Aston Villa finished twenty-second.

Gary says: 'Don't think of it as relegation, think of it as another chance for promotion – how many clubs can look forward to that every other season?'

It was at this point that the 'Swales out' campaign really started to pick up momentum, but it would be another depressing, wrist-slashing, cat-kicking six more years before Swales understood what the word 'out' actually meant. The fans realised that the team that Swales made was not capable of sustaining top-flight status. For the second time that decade City entered their home away from home and spent, again, two seasons there.

Enter stage-right, Mel Machin, whose turn it was to get the club back into the top flight. There was essentially no money to spend even with selling Paul Stewart to Spurs for £1.7 million (that proves how much debt we were in), and City remained in Division Two for another season, until, in 1989, City finished second and returned to Division One.

There were still five months of the 1980s remaining and yet Swales was to appoint another two managers before the 1990s was to arrive, in spite of defeating United 5-1. At the end of November 1989, City were in free fall once more, propping up all others at the foot of the table. Swales turned once more to Tony Book until he could bring in Howard 'three pints and a whisky chaser' Kendall. Kendall managed to stop the free fall, ending the season in fourteenth place, and, for Swales at least, an extremely frustrating eight-goal difference behind Manchester United, one place above them on the same number of points.

Incidentally, that 5-1 win was made all the more special due to a combination of it being at home, the club only just having been promoted back into the top flight, and that the players who featured that day were worth a grand total of approximately £1.7 million, of which six had come through from the Academy. Manchester United meanwhile, who were sticklers for promoting from within (because that's what they have always done) could only point to Beardsmore and Hughes as 'United through and through', while the rest of the team that day cost a total of £7.75 million. This was the forerunner to their domination during the next two decades – 'we don't buy success' my arse ...

You might ask whether there anything else of note during this patch. Not much, since you were asking. City got to the final of the newly introduced Full Member's Cup in 1986, playing against Chelsea at Wembley. The only trouble was, City who had just played a League game against Manchester United a mere 24 hours beforehand, didn't actually start playing until several minutes before the final whistle, when they were already down 5-1. Realising there was an actual game of football being played, with the possibility of a trophy, City scored three times in 5 minutes – if only they'd woken up a couple of minutes earlier.

Swales managed to get a new sponsor in the form of Brother (after changing from Saab to Philips) in 1987, which lasted for three years and was worth a staggering £500,000. Impressive, yes, but when the millions of debt was taken into account, it amounted to essentially nothing. This was due to spending an unprecedented £9.1 million in ten seasons (upwards of £12 million if you include player swaps), even though Swales was repeatedly heard saying 'we have been overcharged with players, but we won't do that again.'

Of course there was that thing with the building of a new roof ... Maine Road had hardly been touched over the years, or at least touched by anyone who gave a damn. It was loved by the fans, but loved in the sort of way you loved your small teddy bear as a small child, which now looked more like something the dog had coughed up. It was a hodgepodge of a stadium with some original aspects of the 1920s mixed up with 1980s duct tape, and a good smattering of all the horrors and pleasures of every intervening decade. The roof above the main stand was replaced – with Swales declaring it cost £1 million at every opportunity that presented itself – but there had been other plans that would have cost at least another £5 million, including, quite staggeringly, a helicopter landing pad (Swales was determined to build an 'evil headquarters'), but a couple of relegations into Division Two soon knocked that idea on the head.

There was one rather interesting event that ironically happened during 'the patch'; City had the best goals-to-minutes player ever, and at the time the youngest ever player (seventeen years and eighty-three days) to score in the club's history (until Marcos Lopes broke that record in January 2013). Please step forward, Ian Thompstone.

Who? Forget your Tommy Johnstones, Sergio Agüeros, Neil Youngs, and Billy Merediths of this world – Ian Thompstone beat them all.

Saturday 9 April, *v.* Middlesbrough away. With 20 minutes to go, Thompstone came on, replacing Trevor Morley, and then duly scored. He never played again. 20 minutes and one goal. No one in the history of our club has ever come close to besting that – it was all very 1890s.

Finally, and thankfully, the patch came to a close. Suffice to say that the entire decade had been an unmitigated disaster. No trophies and no money, yet the City faithful just kept turning up at an increasingly dilapidated, cannabis-smoke-filled, urine-smelling Maine Road. Swales was still in charge, and point-blank refused to leave the club.

It couldn't get any worse. Could it?

Happy Birthday Manchester City!
16 April

2-0 *v.* West Ham.
Hey! 'The patch' wasn't so bad after all.

'We Are Not, We're Not Really Here' Chant

Reason 1: Luton Town bans all away fans after rioting Millwall supporters, yet Manchester City fans still manage to get into the ground in large numbers for an away fixture between the two sides and celebrate this fact by singing that they are not really there.

Reason 2: With the football so awful, but unable to stop themselves from attending, the City fans sang that they were not really there to witness the awfulness. This created a paradox, as the fans would have to be there not to be there. MIT of Massachusetts currently offers a doctorate discussing the ramifications to the equilibrium of time due to the Maine Road faithful.

How Awesome Were City in the 1980s?

Record for most home defeats in a row: 5
Record for the longest run without a win: 17
Record for the longest run at home without a win: 9
Record for the longest run away without a win: 34
Record for the most inflatable bananas popped in exasperation in one game: 3,642

What Was 'the Fifth Column'?

Contrary to popular belief, you don't actually need four other columns – just the one will do – but 'Oneth Column' never sounded right, so fifth it was then.

You know when you're doing something at home and your wife suggests you are doing it all wrong and that her mother could help you out? Yes, it was something like that.

At City there was much talk of a group of people within and without of the club who spent their entire day trying to undermine the management of the club; it was these people who were the 'Fifth Column'. Trouble was, no one knew who these people were or indeed why they were doing it. Some asked if they even existed, but these sane and sensible people were ridiculed. 'Can you prove they don't exist? No, thought not. What? Prove they do exist? How can I do that when they don't want to be discovered? I dunno, some people can be complete idiots at times.

One could surmise of course that the Fifth Column was actually unintentionally created by the people who claimed that the Fifth Column existed, much like throwing sand on to the road every day to ensure tigers don't roam the streets.[7]

Frank Clark and Joe Royle even mentioned it during two separate interviews, so it must be true, right? But if so, who were they?

Actually, I can't tell you, because no one knows. Worst. Chapter. Ever.

Notable Players of the 1980s

Trevor Francis, 1981–82

If a lesson was needed in how to waste money, one need only look at the £1.2 million spent and twenty-six games played for player Trevor Francis. Apparently the lesson was not learned by some fans who wanted him back, as seen when City were in Division Two and had even less money. At least we got a really nice roof though.

Ian Brightwell, 1982–98

Brightwell was a charmed character; he must have been. He survived at the club during some of its darkest hours, saw no less than thirteen different managers during his professional career, ruptured his right knee to put him out of the game for over a year, and went through the horrors of Swales and Mr Chairman, all culminating in a lucrative testimonial match. Either that or he had some seriously juicy gossip about the board of directors.

Eric Nixon, 1983–88

Goalkeeper Nixon is renowned for playing for four different clubs in all four divisions in one season, after being sent out on loan four times by Manchester City. City responded in the 1990s by attempting to do the same sort of thing spread out over four seasons.

Neil McNab, 1983–90

This fella moved twice before arriving at City, both times for around a quarter of a million. City got him for £35,000. One of the (very) few occasions City did something on the cheap and got right.

Mick McCarthy, 1983–87
This English/Irish/Yorkshireman hybrid famously scored a header against Manchester United that was hit so hard it actually gained orbit, and now follows a similar route to that of the International Space Station.

Paul Moulden, 1984–89
This diminutive striker entered the Guinness Book of Records after scoring 8,000 goals at Bolton for the U15s in just one season. I'll have some of that, thought Swales, only to realise later that the opposition City were facing were professionals in their twenties and thirties.

Paul Lake, 1987–1992
Praise could not be given enough to Lakey from the City faithful, but when surgery was required, instead of the *Six Million Dollar Man*, Swales gave us the Eight Quid Fifty Man.

Thanks for that.

Trevor Morley, 1988–89
You know how some players just seem to fit into a side? Morley was one such player. Guided us to promotion on the final day of the 1989 season, he began the 5-1 route of Manchester United the following season. Irreplaceable, yes? Actually, no. Also had a minor problem with people occasionally stabbing him in bed.

Ian Bishop, 1989 (and 1998–2001)
He had been at Everton but Howard Kendall sold him, with Bishop eventually ending up at City. Unfortunately for Bish, Howard Kendall arrived at the Blues and promptly sold him. He returned nine years later with the knowledge that his arch-nemesis, Kendall, was never going to return.

Rumour has it, they bumped into each other at a local grocery store, whereby Kendall attempted to sell him to an elderly lady waiting in line at the check-out.

A Manchester City Fan of the 1980s Has His Say

Name: Colin Davis
Age: 27
First City game ever attended: Some piece of crap in 1982

Laugh or cry – some days I just don't know what to do. Me mam says I shouldn't be putting me self through all this hassle. 'But it's City, mam, I can't help it,' I says to her.

Mind you, I spend most afternoons in the Kippax watching the lads, while completely tanked up – sorta numbs the pain, if you get where I'm going – so, never really sure whether they're playing well or not. Better to be safe than sorry, huh? Always mad for it though.

Mind you, I can't keep up with who the manager is these days; how many have we had so far?

How many? So who do we have this week? Oh, you're kidding me! Right, that's that then, better get to the pub an hour earlier than normal.

Swales? Look, mate, I'm not normally a violent guy – usually too drunk, y'see – but the less said about him the better, as far as I am concerned.

Look, I gotta go, kick-off is in 7 hours, and I'm way too sober. It's gonna be a top banana today … I hope.

---

1 Other than suffering from internal bleeding, strokes and cancer of the liver due to the amount of anti-depressants being taken to combat the shoddiness.
2 Which, by its very nature, means the guy was awesome.
3 Read: Divine Intervention.
4 Perhaps we need another one. Just saying.
5 Randy buggers are them Scotsmen.
6 To be fair, Pompey haven't had anything to laugh about for quite some time.
7 That really works, you know.

WHY, YES, I DO ENJOY PLAYING AGAINST MACCLESFIELD TOWN

The 1970s and the '80s for City had been a bit of a 'crazy train' affair – they had lifted a Cup, been in Europe, but they had also been relegated more than once. Still, entering the 1990s and, after hammering United 5-1 in 1989,[1] the fans could look forward to a decade of much greater success, especially with all this talk of a new 'super-league' in England, because City were deemed to be one of the current big clubs. This was irrespective of the fact that City had just experienced the worst ten years in their history – or perhaps it was just City deeming themselves as one of the big clubs.

The club had been part of those pushing for the formation of a Premiership League and Peter Swales was heard explaining that the age of a £3 million player and contracts of £7,000 a week was coming. However, Colin Bell wrote in a match day programme that he wanted the Football League to remain as it was, and that to change it could cost the club dear.[2]

However, quite unbelievably, the seasons ending in 1991 and 1992 saw the club finish fifth, with the latter being the last season before the English top flight was changed forever (and also the last season when fans could guarantee that their team would be playing at 3 p.m. on a Saturday). This was despite Howard Kendall leaving to bugger off back to Everton where he had previously been in charge, only to leave for Athletic Bilbao when English clubs were banned from Europe. This ban was removed in 1990/91, so why he came to City first, is anyone's guess.[3]

Hyde Road

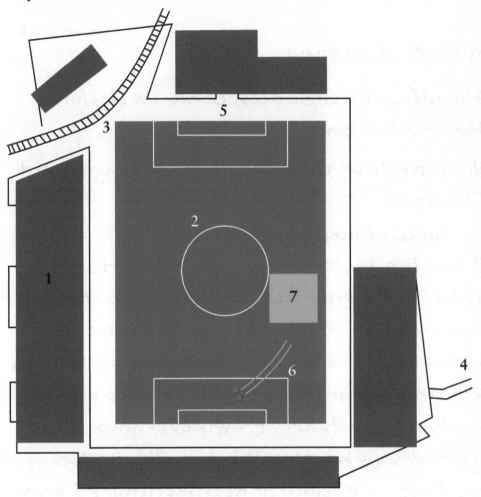

1. Please smoke anywhere but here.
2. Pitch is for illustrative purposes only. It was not this green.
3. Taking a corner precisely 3.27 p.m. on Saturday was not advised.
4. Alleyway to homes (mostly players') and, more importantly, the pub.
5. OAP and child access for ease-of-use pitch invasion.
6. Tyre marks of a Crossley 20/25. Defender James McNeal of Aston Villa got in the way – Max Woosman wins City a penalty!
7. King George V stood right here – this pitch of grass is worth more than entire stadium.

21st Feb. 1981

Minutes of meeting

Attending: Peter Swales, Benhard Halford, ~~James~~ John Bond

Not attending: Granada TV and their stupid filmcrew

Topic of meeting: TOP SECRET!!!

JB wants a bigger transfer ~~budget~~, BH shakes his head, PS promises not to laugh but doesn't quite make it. PS discusses where the club should be at the end of the season, JB suggests 12th and a trip to Wembley. BH asks where the choc biscuits are, PS wipes crumbs from face and says he doesn't know. BH ~~suggests~~ introduction of cake to next meeting. PS grins because we just beat United. JB is also happy but doesn't understand what the fascination is with United. BH shakes his head again, but PS doesn't notice as he is too busy grinning but then begins to glare at JB with an emphasis of evil in it. Meeting ends.

Etihad Stadium

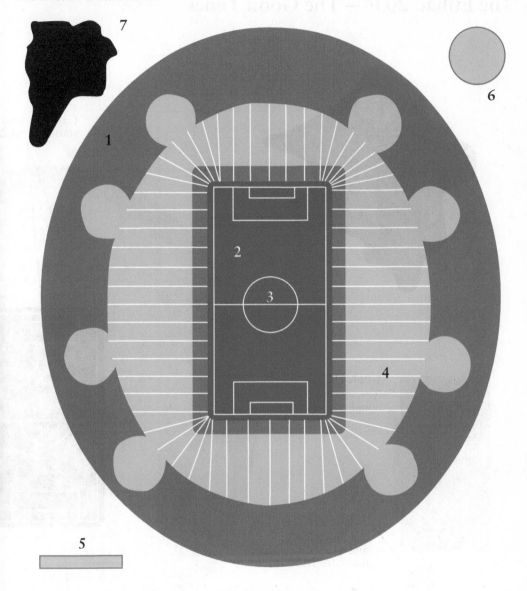

1. Much like the Nazca lines of Chile, when viewed from miles up, the stadium takes on the appearance of a ... umm ... bug.
2. Graphical representation of pitch does not do it justice. Seriously people, it's like angels have come down from Heaven and done some weeding.
3. Buried Barcelona shirt (put there by Barcelona).
4. Distinct lack of copper piping (removed by local residents).
5. Proposed Metrolink station.
6. Proposed docking platform from private spaceships.
7. Location of fourth largest oil field in the world discovered in 2007.

The Etihad 2034 – The Good Times

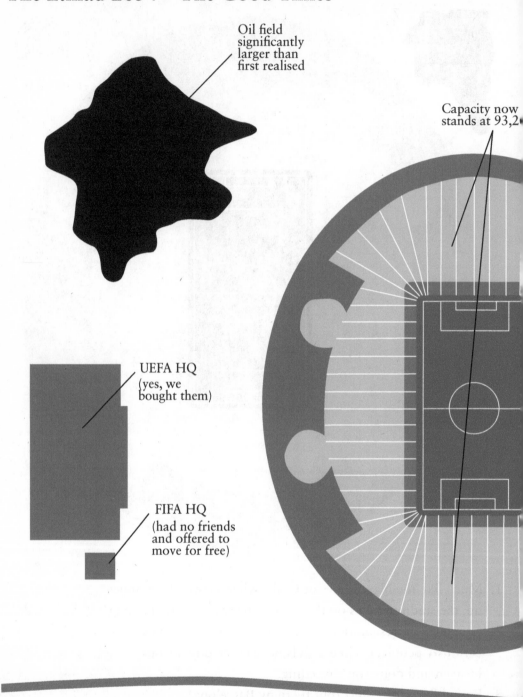

Oil field significantly larger than first realised

Capacity now stands at 93,2(

UEFA HQ
(yes, we bought them)

FIFA HQ
(had no friends
and offered to
move for free)

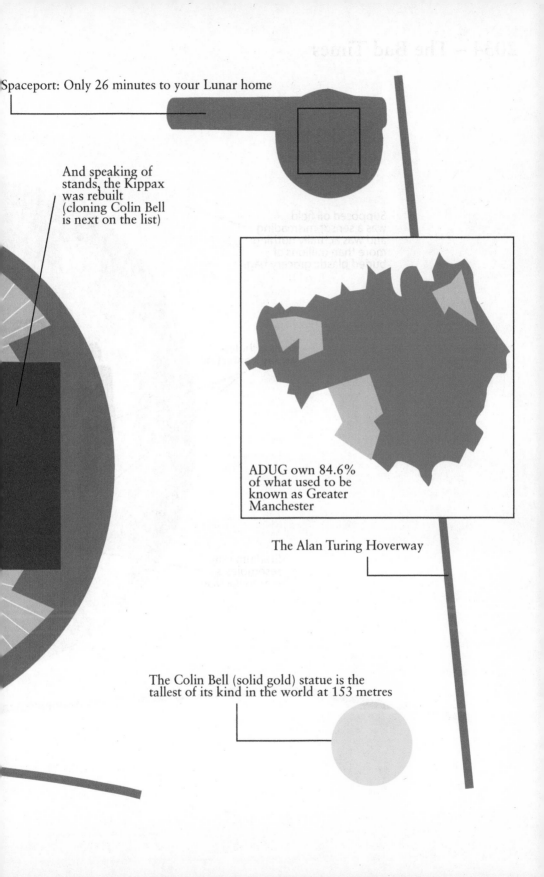

Spaceport: Only 26 minutes to your Lunar home

And speaking of stands, the Kippax was rebuilt (cloning Colin Bell is next on the list)

ADUG own 84.6% of what used to be known as Greater Manchester

The Alan Turing Hoverway

The Colin Bell (solid gold) statue is the tallest of its kind in the world at 153 metres

2034 – The Bad Times

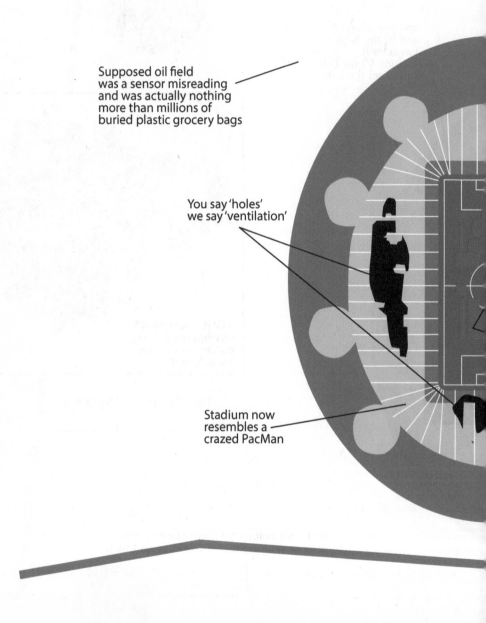

Supposed oil field was a sensor misreading and was actually nothing more than millions of buried plastic grocery bags

You say 'holes' we say 'ventilation'

Stadium now resembles a crazed PacMan

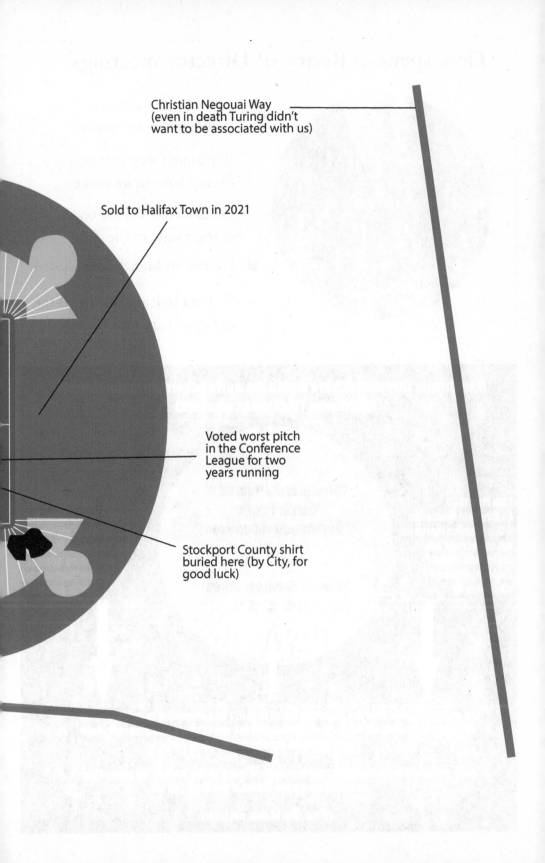

Christian Negouai Way
(even in death Turing didn't
want to be associated with us)

Sold to Halifax Town in 2021

Voted worst pitch
in the Conference
League for two
years running

Stockport County shirt
buried here (by City, for
good luck)

Time spent in Board of Director meetings

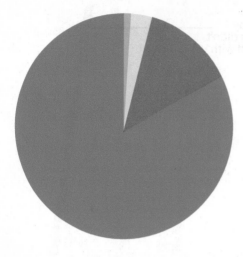

- Listening to manager asking for more money

- Explaining why manager cannot have more money

- Constructive debate on the current state of the club

- Hating on Manchester United

- Waiting to leave due to all the unhappy City fans outside

Manchester City should have ended the world according to the Mayans (but Martin Tyler saves mankind)

13th May 1963
As City beat Newcastle 4-3, a massive march on the streets of Paris protesting against authoritiarianism was going on

The sun is distracted by Martin Tyler's "Aguerooooooooooooo!"

Planet Earth breathes a sigh of relief

13th May 1963
As City beat Newcastle 4-3, a massive march on the streets of Moscow protesting against authoritiarianism was going on

The number of days between these two dates is 16,071, that according to the Mayans is the exact number of 'bits' to pass culminating in the sun to change its magnetic field leading to the destruction of Planet Earth.

Also, either authoritiarianism is not appreciated much by the masses, oir protesting about it is a very good thing if you are a City fan.

On the 13th of May, obviously.

It is interesting to note that Swales kept saying the club had no money for anything (ask Paul Lake, he'll tell you), yet in March 1990 he paid £900,000 for Niall Quinn, in July paid a club record £1 million for 'keeper Tony Coton, and thirteen months later paid £2.5 million to make Keith Curle the most expensive defender in the country.[4]

Actually, Mr Disco Pants and Coton became big favourites with the City support, particularly the former, who once famously went in between the sticks after Coton had been sent off versus Derby County in April of 1991, and was called upon to save a penalty, which he then duly did, relegating Derby County in the process. Coton never returned the favour by scoring though and then buggered off to Manchester United for half of what City had initially paid. Yeesh.

As ever, the 'Swales out!' campaign continued unabated, but something was to happen in May 1991 that retrospectively speaking was not ideal – Manchester City finished above Manchester United. Peter Reid was now at the helm as player-manager after arriving in November of 1990, and had managed to achieve Swales' dream for the first time since 1977/78. No number of calls for Swales to step down were going to shift him now; it was going to take something extraordinary to remove him. Reid repeated the success of finishing in fifth place the following season, but this time United finished in second and were also re-admitted into European competition.

In 1992, the Premiership (and therefore football itself) finally arrived – loud, proud, and heralding the potential of creating the greatest league in the world. Much to Swales' dismay, not only did City drop to ninth that season, but he also saw Manchester United win the damn thing. Additionally, even Nottingham Forest, who finished bottom, managed to score more goals than City had. It was something that needed to be addressed for the next season if City were going to have any chance of finishing near the top. Only thing was though, they didn't, and somehow managed to score even less, finishing bottom for the second season in a row in the 'Goals For' table. In what must have seemed like a stroke of genius to Swales, he had removed Reid and Ellis after earning just one point from the first four games in this new campaign, and brought in the world-renowned powerhouse that was Brian Horton. Reid went back to just playing football at Southampton, while still being paid by City to the tune of around £2,000 a week. I wonder how long we'll be paying him for?

But the 1993/94 season was not actually about football (which was just as well, as the City faithful were barely getting anything that one could describe as football), as there were far more important comings and goings at the club. Twenty years, eleven sackings, and after more bad decisions than you could shake a large novelty-sized banana at, Peter Swales was out.

Sydney, Australia, was selected to be the host of the 2000 Summer Olympics, the European Union was formally established, the North American Free Trade Agreement came into effect, Lorena Bobbitt was officially found out to be 'a little crazy' and Peter Reid was still being paid £2,000 a week – all of this paled into comparison with the removal of Mr Swales at 12.30 a.m. on Saturday 5 February 1994.

The bananas rejoiced and there was much dancing of the yellow fruit, for the saviour of the club – the one who the fans had been pleading for months and months to take control – waltzed in and very much did take control. Francis Lee, the player Peter Swales had sold in 1974, had come back to Maine Road and had finally ousted the most hated figure at Maine Road – except, of course, when Alex Ferguson brought his team over once a year. How bad is it that one needs their own hated figure to make an appearance to be given a day off from being the most hated?[5]

The 'Forward with Franny' campaign had been gaining ground for quite some time and most cunning it had been too, as Lee had essentially let everyone else do all the campaigning for him; even the national media threw their weight in behind him. He rarely came to City games either, only showing up to receive the adoration from the masses once he knew he was close to the finishing line.[6]

Swales hated Lee, quite possibly even more than he hated Manchester United.[7] He knew that if there was anyone in this world who could remove him, it was Lee. He tried to find another buyer – a rich Mancunian, some other ex-player, a foreign investment company, anyone, just anyone. There had been rumours of possible buyers who would invest massive amounts of money into the club, which made

Swales extremely happy, but all had walked away once they realized how much support Lee had.

So Peter Swales finally lost the unwavering support of all the major shareholders and the power he had loved and craved throughout the past years was ripped away from him. He walked away a bruised and battered, tired and broken man. Manchester City had been saved![8]

The only trouble was that Lee was just as bad, if not worse, than Swales.[9] Sure, he was quite likeable, what with being an ex-player and all, but soon after his appointment the club fell into the pit of Hades, and made the 1980s look like a successful decade.

As a player, Franny was held in the highest regard and after retiring from the game he earned a few pennies selling toilet paper, then used £3 million of his 'dirty' money to buy the club.[10]

Manchester City would be the happiest club in the land and, I suppose, at that very precise moment in time, it was. With promises of £50 million to spend and the legendary Franz Beckenbauer to take the manager's position, what could possibly go wrong? Swales was gone. The hero had ridden into town and conquered all before him. He even conquered the legend who is Colin Bell, by letting Frank Clark tell him 'You're sacked.' Fantastic stuff … hang on, WHAT?

It was only a few months into the reign of Franny that some fans began to question what he was doing. City had a massive wage bill at £5.5 million – the biggest in the club's existence – and while it was recognised that something had to be done about it, those who were shipped out were not directly replaced. It was akin to knowing that your big car was running your wallet dry, so you replaced it with a bucket.

There was talk of players like Matt Le Tissier, David Platt and Dennis Bergkamp being looked at and considered, but ultimately nothing came of it. Bergkamp, huh? Silly Arsenal. The best Franny could do was get Gaudino in on loan from Frankfurt, after his coach, Jupp Heynckes, had told him to find a new club for the rest of the season because he had refused to turn up for a match. Oh, and at the time he was a suspect in a car-theft ring. And he was to cost the club £200,000. Plus £3,000 a week. Brilliant.

Despite offloading players, which everyone realised Franny had to do, at the end of 1994 City posted a record near £6 million loss.

Naturally, Franny blamed Swales, the £2,000-a-week Reid was still getting and that the club had only narrowly avoided relegation the previous season – better hope we do better this season then, or will that be the previous chairman's fault, too?

CHICKENS!

During 1994 and the beginning of 1995, a recognisable new fan was seen at every home game, and he went by the name of Frankie. Frankie was a chicken. And a dead one at that. He applauded and waved on the team, and was apparently a massive Uwe Rösler fan, joining in with the singing.

A vegetarian City fan complained about Frankie and from that moment Frankie got a lifetime ban from attending all City matches. Hitler was a vegetarian, too. Just saying.

Franny decided to leave Horton in charge (obviously Beckenbauer was on holiday or something), even though there were rumours of secret meetings with Ron Atkinson. This paid off massive dividends, even with a war chest of a supposed £10 million given to him (this is obviously very close to the value of £50 million) when City dropped to sixteenth and then seventeenth. What was particularly nerve-wracking for the fans was that the Premier League had stated that the 1994/95 season would see four teams and not the usual three be relegated into Division One, with only two coming the opposite way, due to the League wanting to reduce the number of clubs from twenty-two down to twenty. City clung on by a mere four points.

City were desperate for money – far more desperate than the fans realised – but then in came an offer from Sporting Lisbon for Niall Quinn to the tune of £1.5 million. While this would not have solved everything (not even close), it certainly would have helped. What didn't help was that Quinny was owed money from the club, but he was refused a cut of the transfer fee. A few days of haggling later and City ended up with nothing and Quinn was still on the City books.

Going back to Horton, he was not one of Lee's buddies and so after a second horrible season in charge, he was sacked and replaced. 'Beckenbauer?', asked the fans, 'He's no longer manager at Bayern München.' 'Well, his last name starts with a B,' replied Franny.

At one point, City could have had the League's first ever chairman-manager, as he stated he was prepared to take over both roles. However, who would have been able to fire him, if it all went tits-up? It would have actually been pretty bloody impressive, though, because when everyone is already laughing at the club, one must up one's game to find a new funny.

Live Life Like a New Chairman

Tell your family how awesome you are by promising to take them on an all-inclusive five-week cruise in the Bahamas.

Do not consider the possibilities of what will happen when they actually end up at a crummy B&B in Bognor Regis for a rain-soaked weekend.

City's 172nd manager stepped up to the plate in the form of Alan 'I have a job that is the envy of millions' Ball, who brought in ex-City Asa Hartford as his assistant. He was very good friends with Francis Lee and had apparently been promised the job prior to him becoming chairman, so why it took so soddin' long to hire him is anyone's guess.[11] The author has just realized that Mr Lee insisted upon everyone calling him 'Mr Chairman', so that's what's going to happen from now on; sincerest apologies, Mr Chairman. Actually, prior to Ball being appointed, Dave Bassett, who was at Crystal Palace at the time, had agreed to everything, including a player to sign with Mr Chairman, only to get cold feet overnight. Mr Chairman was not best pleased upon being told this over the phone by Bassett and explained he would thrash him the next time he came to Maine Road. As it turned out it was a well deserved 1-1 thrashing, with Palace winning at their place 3-1, which helped them get into the play-offs and ultimately into the Premier League. That'd teach him to turn down Mr Chairman.

Ball had been at Southampton and the appointment was not well received by the Saints' fans, nor by the Southampton board who demanded £500,000 from City. Around the same time, Horton began legal proceedings against the club to the tune of £200,000 (he didn't end up getting it though), and Peter Reid was still getting his £2,000 a week for not being there. Did I mention we hadn't signed anyone yet? At least we knew some money was on its way in the shape of Gerry Taggart – he had been at City from 1989/90 only to be sold to Barnsley for £75,000. Swales, however, had insisted on a 50 per cent sell-on clause should Barnsley get tired of him. Five years later, City raked in £750,000 – thank you very much Bolton Wanderers. I doubt Mr Chairman thanked Swales though.

Before the 199/96 season started, Mr Chairman proudly stated that he had got his house completely in order; the debts were all gone, and they owed nothing to any club for previous transfer deals. Profits would be rolling in, the team could be improved, and the club and fans could look forward to a healthy and prosperous future.

In the job that was apparently the envy of millions, the prosperous future Mr Chairman was not to win a game for the first three months of the season and managed a team that scored only three goals.[12] Somehow though, Ball won the Manager of the Month award for November (no, seriously, he did).

By Christmas 1995, reports were surfacing that City were now in debt to the tune of £19 million. But how could this be? Mr Chairman had said that the club was debt-free just five months before.

Mr Chairman had, however, brought in a diminutive Georgian by the name of Kinkladze, for what was proved to be an absolute bargain price of £2 million. Rumours did persist that he didn't cost anywhere close to that and it was more Mr Chairman allegedly bigging up the numbers. Kinky's centre of gravity was so low that the University of Manchester scientifically proved it was impossible to knock him over and that, coupled with actually knowing what to do with a football once at his feet (i.e. don't pass it to any of his teammates), he created some sublime moments for the City faithful. Even if it took a while for him to initially get going, when he did he scored The Greatest Goal Ever Scored In The World Of Goals Scored

Ever versus Southampton in March of '96. Sadly, Joe Royle thought the opposite of what everyone else thought about Kinkladze.

As said, in 1993/94 we finished sixteenth, followed by seventeenth in 1994/95, so no one should have been shocked that at the end of 1995/96 we finished in eighteenth place. At least we had finally stopped paying Peter Reid though. Sadly we couldn't go for nineteenth the next season as we were, once again, back in the second tier, due to the League now only having twenty teams. Although this was now called Division One, which undoubtedly was causing confusion on the City board of directors.

Several games into the 1995/96 season, it was quite obvious to all that the writing was not just on the wall, but also on the floor and ceiling. After initially drawing against Spurs on the opening day 1-1, City then went on to lose the next eight matches, only scoring in two of them. By the end of October, City were rockbottom on one point and a -18 goal difference. It wasn't until 4 November that the first win of the season had been recorded at home to Bolton Wanderers, and it wasn't until New Year's Day that City managed to score more than once in a match.

Three days before the final game of the season of 1995/96 (where it was deemed to be a good idea to draw versus Liverpool), Peter Swales died in Wythenshaw Hospital. City fans should have seen this as a sign of impending doom – he may have been hated, but he had loved the club in his own way (perhaps too much), and he was buggered if he was going to watch the club get relegated again. 'Nope. You asked for Lee and now you've got him. I'm outta here.' Surprisingly, in what was a nice touch, the City faithful gave Swales a minute's silence before kick-off, although part of that minute was probably for the benefit of the team on the pitch.

It was during the summer that clubs started sniffing around a lot of the City players (seems sensible to buy up much of the squad that had just been relegated) and Norwegian multi-millionaires, Rokke and Gjelsten, wanted to buy the club outright. They failed, and ended up buying Wimbledon FC. So that went well then.

Somehow, Ball managed to last a little longer, with Mr Chairman hiding him under his desk, but he was soon to be replaced by a string of managers – Steve Coppell, Frank Clark, the guy who delivered the newspaper, Richard Edgehill's mother and, finally, ex-City player Joe Royle. It was hardly surprising City dropped to fourteenth in Division One the next season, but they were closer to the play-offs, points wise, than the relegation spots. Often the team would play diabolically, but because this was no longer the top-flight, they somehow got away with it. Off the pitch, debts were increasing, vultures were circling, but shares were increasing in value – it was all very strange. At the beginning of the 1996/97 season, City went forty-two days without a proper manager before Steve Coppell arrived. The Official Supporter's Club wanted stability above all else, and so planned Operation Get Behind Our Manager; unfortunately it took thirty-four days to start it.

During the months of November and December, City had eleven League games, and lost eight of them, so this might explain why Mr Chairman felt it was necessary to bugger off to the Caribbean. Conversely, once he was back, City lost only four more times all season; I suppose that gave Mr Chairman all the reason he needed for interfering with the manager's team-tactics-talk.

The FA Reiterates that Manchester United Are Not in Manchester

The 1996 European Championship was held in England, and several stadia were selected to be used throughout the tournament. Naturally being the largest club stadium, Old Trafford was chosen.

The FA then handed out grants to various councils to help them cope with extra costs they might incur from hundreds of thousands of visiting fans. Manchester Council received £30,000, but Trafford Council didn't get a single penny, even though they and not Manchester were hosting matches.

The season of 1997/98 would be the one to see us back in the top flight, but the fans, after suffering for twenty years under Swales, had already cottoned on to Mr Chairman and knew that what had been said and, in my opinion, this promise basically amounted to pure, unadulterated bullshit. Mr Chairman did point to the £13 million spent on the new stand and that we were virtually a Premier League side – I suppose we also virtually drew all those games we lost by one goal.

3 May 1998 will go down in history as the day that the world officially ended (everything since then has just been a figment of our imagination). In true typical City fashion, they had just convincingly beaten Stoke City away, 5-2, but it didn't matter, as both Portsmouth and Port Vale won their games. The trapdoor opened and for the first time in the club's 118-year history, Manchester City entered the third tier of English football.

In actuality, it was the match preceding that one that had sealed the club's fate and everything about it screamed 'Typical City' until it was blue in the face. Jamie Pollock scored a grand total of five goals from sixty appearances for the club – not too shabby for a defensive midfielder – but it was his 'goal of a lifetime' against Queens Park Rangers that left everyone stunned.

The ball was flicked in from the right-wing near the penalty area, with Pollock gracefully catching it with his right foot, lifting it over defender's heads. With still the onrushing 'keeper to beat, Pollock kept his stride in check with the ball and met it perfectly as it came back down with his head. The 'keeper could do nothing as the power and trajectory of the ball left him completely stranded; a sublime individual piece of skill that any player in the world would be proud of. Trouble was, it was against his own teammates.

Never before had anyone witnessed an own goal of such magnitude. There had been plenty of freak happenings before; an unfortunate deflection, a volley from outside the area that was intended to put the ball in row-Z, a last ditch tackle that at any other time would have seen the player kick the ball out of play. This was none of those.

Pollock eventually retired from professional football at the tender age of twenty-eight – no one outside of non-League football would touch him. Still, at least it saved QPR's skin and kept them in League One – they owe us big time. Don't you worry Rangers, we'll be back later to collect.

Earlier that season, Mr Chairman had made a very bold statement to the fans – he would jump off from the top of the Kippax if City were relegated into the third division. Suffice to say, this never happened. Or at least I never heard about it happening.

The City faithful were staring in disbelief at the unfolding horror. But could all this have been avoided? In 1996, Prince Walid Ibn Galal of Saudi Arabia was rumoured to be interested in purchasing the club and investing in it to the tune of £75 million (he had already come to the rescue of Euro Disney). This was a mere three years after Mr Chairman had bought control for £3 million. The Prince eventually walked away due to the accounts books being hidden from him, instead shown a napkin with the words 'couldn't be better' scribbled on it. There was talk of Dave Whelan and his mega millions, but due to the financial state of the club, he ran off too. This obviously meant that the club was in a bigger mess than the country of Greece, *c.* 2012.[13]

It should be noted, however, that even though the club was at times closer to the Unibond League than the Premiership, City still recorded huge attendances, but this was because, in part, to the fact that the fans were gluttons for punishment and that beating oneself with a leather strap just wasn't cutting it any more.

Mr Chairman realized that he had to go, and quickly and quietly shuffled off before the 1997/98 season had finished, leaving the fans fuming, but at the same time thankful that he had not done a Swales and locked himself in his office with his fingers in his ears. Up stepped life-long City fan David Bernstein, who had previously been the financial director. Quite why no one questioned the philosophy of promoting someone in charge of looking after the money we had consistently wasted is anyone's guess.

Funnily enough, while we were at our lowest, with cash reserves now equating to questions of 'You haven't got change for a quid, have you?', Manchester City embarked upon a new venture – a new and improved Manchester City Academy. In 1997 they hit upon the idea that should things go completely pear-shaped, they'd need all the money they could get their hands on, and while it was illegal to print your own money (someone at the club asked, just in case the law had changed), what they could do was create their own footballers and then sell them. Calling in

Jim Cassell, who at the time was chief scout at local Oldham Athletic, he was tasked with building this for the club and, in 1998, it opened for business ... sorry, its doors. Staggeringly, there were actually one or two players who actually made it into the first team.

For those in the know (everyone), the season of 1998/99 was a do or die season. Win and City would survive; lose and Hyde FC was going to gain a hell of a lot of fans. Those 'a hell of a lot of fans' numbered 32,000 for the first game of the season versus Blackpool – reputed to be the second highest crowd attendance in the entire country. Bloody plastics.

It is well known that Manchester City holds the official record for the highest attendance at home for a football match, which still stands to this day. What is not well known is that the club also hold the highest unofficial record attendance as well – 3,629,401.

That staggering figure was accomplished on 19 December 1998 at York City away. Ask your fellow Blues if they were there that day, and they are likely to say 'yes', even if they weren't even born then. In fact this author believes he is the only Blue who wasn't there that day – I am really sorry, Blues. Totally letting the side down.

The month of February, the 13th to be exact – a Saturday for the pedantics out there, saw City travel to the south coast of England to play against Bournemouth.[14] Referee, Brian Coddington, seemed to be determined to book every single City player he could – including subs – throwing in a second yellow card for Pollock just for good measure. Coddington wasn't finished there though, and while Weaver was down on the ground receiving treatment for a clash of heads, he decided now would be an ideal time to book a couple more City players; why not? Play had stopped and he had to do something to pass the time. Horlock, however, stepped in and diffused the situation going on between his fellow Blues and the man in black, then turned and proceeded to move towards the referee. Before he had reached Coddington, the ref produced Horlock's second yellow of the match and sent him off for walking in an aggressive manner.

How City managed to put out a team for their next match against Macclesfield Town, or how Coddington was allowed to continue officiating is unsure, but both somehow managed it. The latter, however, fortunately never stepped onto a pitch as an official after the season ended, not that City minded, or indeed anyone else. Just ask Curbishley's Charlton side in 1997, or McFarlan's Cambridge United side in 1997, or Whitley's 50-yard goal for Wrexham in 1999, or Dario Gradi's Crewe side in 1996, or...

May 1999 saw City compete in arguably their most important game in their 119-year history when they faced Gillingham at Wembley in the play-off final for a chance to enter Division One.[15] City had recently beaten them away in the League 2-0, ending their long unbeaten home record, so the fans were feeling slightly optimistic about the match. However, with barely minutes left on the clock, City were suddenly down 2-0 and the club was effectively doomed. The fans knew it was over, and one by one they slowly made their way out of the stadium.

But then, Kevin Horlock managed to pull one back and, in the dying seconds, up stepped Paul Dickov to blast the ball past the best man at his wedding. Wembley erupted and those who had left raced back into the stadium. Fans won't do that again, will they?

Extra time and penalties came and went before Nicky Weaver beckoned his teammates to follow him and then ran around like a headless chicken after it became clear City were promoted. A remarkable game that City fans said afterwards the likes of it would never, ever, be repeated again. Tony Pulis has never forgiven us for it though.

City broke a record that day, too, which due to the fact that the Wembley of that day only stood for another couple of years, was never beaten – they had packed in more fans than any other club had ever managed to do for one match at that stadium. Third division clubs, huh?

The 1990s were over. We had somehow survived them, even with the 'help' of Swales and Mr Chairman. The club was perilously close to bankruptcy, but at least we now had someone in the chairman's role who looked like he might actually get something done. There was still a long way to go to get back into the top tier – a league we helped form I might add – but there were no guarantees, or at least good guarantees. A new decade and century beckoned; the only way was up.[16]

Let's Play the Richard Edgill Game

Gather some of your work colleagues together, and then choose one person who is happy to be working there and gives their all to the job in hand (they'll be smiling a lot). They will be your Richard Edgill for the day.

Spend the next 90 minutes hurling as much abuse at them as possible (the more personal, the better), as loudly as you can. Extra points will be awarded for rhyming songs that all can join in with. See how long they can last before breaking down in tears and leaving. Congratulate yourselves at the end for being total bastards.

As a side note, Manchester City has the terrible performances of the English national side to thank for not going bankrupt in the early 1990s.

In the Euro 1992 games in Sweden, England didn't even get out of the group stage after drawing two and losing one, and were sent home packing immediately. The reason this was so good for City had something to do with an agreement with Wimbledon FC. When the club signed Keith Curle from them, Peter Swales, for reasons that were beyond everyone, agreed to pay Curle's former club tens of thousands of pounds every time he pulled on an England shirt.

Luckily, as it turned out, he was worse than the team itself and every City fan breathed a sigh of relief when he was never ever picked again.[17] However, while Manchester City were doing their utmost to be not the best representation of a professional football club, down the road in the Borough of Trafford, one club actually removed the words 'football club' from their name completely.

In 1998, Manchester United Football Club was changed to 'Manchester United' by Martin Edwards, or more accurately, 'Manchester United PLC'. 'We are so great and fantastic that we don't need no stinking FC.'

What he didn't explain was that FA rules prevented the distribution of profits to shareholders as an FC, but could do so as a public limited company – United were no longer a club, but a fully fledged business with the sole intent of making as much money for the owners as possible (again). Edwards proved this when he sold the club and ran off into the distance with around £90 million. However, over in the US of America, their name had been shortened even more to 'Man U'. Not a football club, but a sports business, thereby admitting that using the word 'Manchester' for all these years had been a little underhanded (finally)! One can only assume that if this path continues they will be eventually known as 'MU' or indeed plain ol' 'M' – which of course is the thirteenth letter of the alphabet, meaning they could go with 艾 instead so that the Taiwanese home support would feel much happier.

1997 saw the introduction of a shiny brand new crest – the one we have today. Where before it had been based upon, and was sometimes an exact copy of, the city of Manchester coat of arms, the new crest utilised other recognisable aspects of life in Manchester such as a golden eagle.

The club had been unable to register the previous crest because it was essentially the crest of the city; that and the fact that Swales had basically given it away, for a nominal fee, to anyone who wanted to make money from it. Mr Chairman was instrumental in the new design, so we have him to blame for those three stars at the top?

However, in a strange Nostradamus-like moment of vision, Mr Chairman accidentally put the icing on the cake when the club was sold eleven years later, in 2008, when he devised our club's new crest. Abu Dhabi's emblem contains a falcon in a very similar pose, along with a central image of a ship, but even they thought the addition of three stars at the top would look dumb.

Happy Birthday Manchester City!
16 April

1-0 *v.* Norwich
1-1 *v.* Norwich
3-1 *v.* Grimsby
Stupid Norwich.

It's the Big Whiteboard Quiz

From the following whiteboards, can you name the manager, and in the case of the fourth one, the match as well? Answers on page 157.

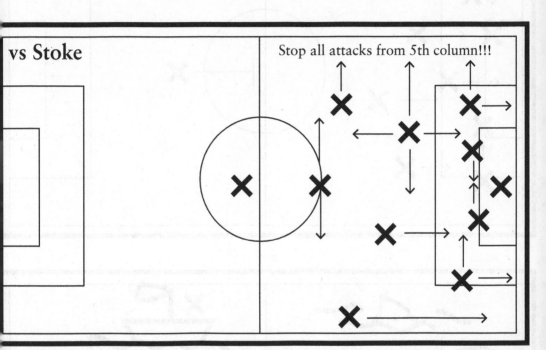

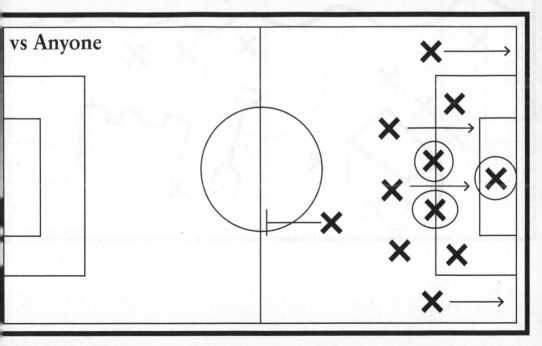

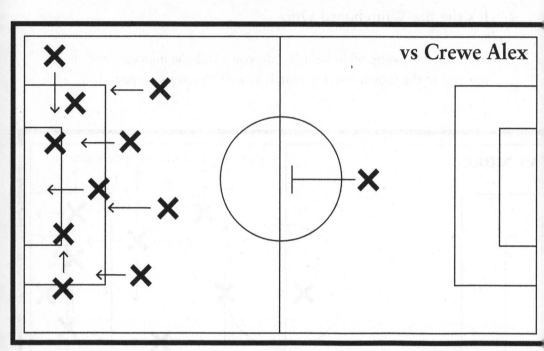

vs Crewe Alex

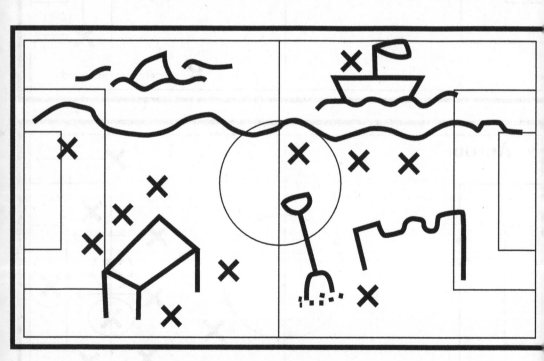

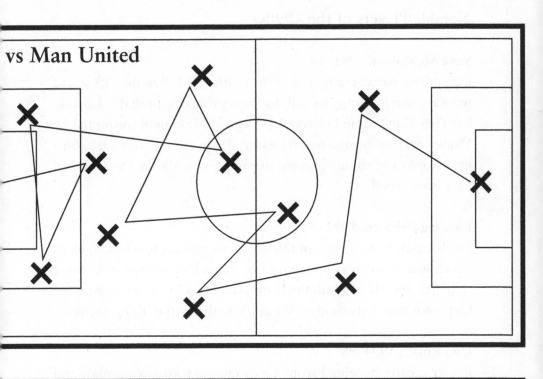

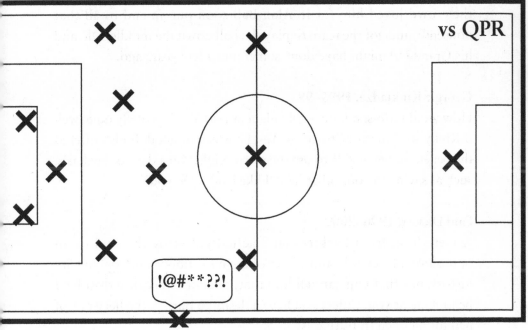

Notable Players of the 1990s

Steve McMahon, 1991–94

Despite the overall crappiness of the 1980s and 1990s, the City squad were a generally happy lot (all that heavy drinking probably helped), but then along came Liverpool FC legend McMahon (respected by Vinnie Jones for being a tough tackler). He pissed on everyone's chips by doing lots of shouting in the dressing room – Mike Doyle would have been proud.

Kåre Ingebrigtsen, 1992–94

Ingebrigtsen had a career of thirteen years playing football, most of which was in Norway – save for one and a half seasons at City for some reason. He also admitted to receiving a bung for signing for City – not from City though! We don't do that sort of thing anymore.

Uwe Rösler, 1994–98

Rösler greatly benefited from City's fast-attacking wing-play, and the crowd loved him for it. Alan Ball soon put an end to all that nonsense, and got the team to play the ball down the middle. Oh, and his Granddad might have done something a few years ago.

Georgie Kinkladze, 1995–98

How would Messi fair on a cold night at Port Vale? Actually quite well if Kinky was anything to go by. Yes, he was that good. It also offered the benefit of being able to use the word 'Kinky' on a day-to-day basis, such as saying to your other-half: 'I like Kinky. Do you?'

Paul Dickov, 1996–2002

A mere look from Dickov could actually destroy the soul of an opposition player. Oh, and scorer of the most important goal in City history, not that you can tell him that, of course, because then he'd be looking at you. Unless you have a desire to burn in the fiery pits of hell for all of eternity, that is.

Andy Morrison, 1998–2001
Bought from Huddersfield Town for a cup of coffee and a curly-wurly, Morrison proved to be, pound for pound, the buy of the century, captaining the side to the Wembley win against Gillingham.

Admittedly, he did have a minor problem with picking up cards, whether they were in the first team or reserve games. He has amassed so big a suspension that the Premier League has banned him from featuring in any competitive game until 16 March 2023.

Shaun Goater, 1998–2003
City's very own *Cool Runnings*, but sadly with no egg to kiss. He holds the Premier League record for scorer of the fastest ever goal by a substitute, timed at just 9 seconds after entering the field of play. Oh, and it was against Manchester United. Also scored 100 goals, with his 100th coming against, yes, that lot, too. He was voted City's Happiest Player for three seasons on the trot.

Robert Taylor, 1999–2000
Bob once scored a wonder goal against Manchester City and almost single-handedly destroyed the club by scoring in the 1999 Division Two play-off final. Obviously it made perfect sense that we signed him for £1.5 million then. It was also obvious that he would turn out to be utterly useless.

A Manchester City Fan of the 1990s Has His Say

Name: Tyrone Davis
Age: 26
First City game ever attended: City *v*. QPR, first season of the Premiership.

It's my Dad's fault. 'But I like rugby!' I tells him. Not havin' any of it though, is he? Drags me along, I get into it, and before you know it, I'm a City fan and now we're absolutely crap. Bastard.

Do I still go? Of course I do, I'm City through and through. Dunno why though. I could be practising more with my band,

The Moonchilds – y'wanna hear our latest one? It's got a bangin' beat; they played it at The Hacienda last weekend. No? Alright suit yourself.

There is one thing though, even though we're shit and stuff, and we're playing at grounds I never dreamed of, we're all still havin' a good laugh; who'd have thought Division One football would be so much fun?

What? Banana? Are you taking the piss?

Oh! Them inflatable things! Sorry, mate … nah, don't go in for that nonsense, although my Dad keeps going on about them giving them racist bastards something to use against us. I keep telling him we should wave a 'How To Dance' book around (laughs).

Hopes? Well, we just finished fourteenth in Division One, but I really can't see us getting any worse than this. So, next season we go for the big push back into the Premiership.

Division Two? Nah, mate, never gonna happen.

Celebrating 100 Years: 16 April 1994

Getting to 100 is an achievement in anyone's book. 100 years means a lot, so much so that a war that lasted 116 years in the fourteenth and fifteenth centuries, is only known as 'The Hundred Years War' – mind you it's doubtful anyone could count in those days.

So in reaching a century, you would celebrate, yes? Push out all the stops, invite everybody, be loud and proud, and generally be a noisy neighbour. This is City though.

Exactly 100 years to the day that Manchester City came into being from the ashes of Ardwick/West Gorton/etc, City took to the pitch at Maine Road and kicked-off *v.* Norwich City. At full time it was 1-1. The (allegedly) 28,010 people that came to see the game went home, did general stuff, went to bed, and awoke the next morning to continue with doing stuff. That was fun.

Actually it wasn't like City didn't do anything at all, because the current mayoress at the time, Shelia Smith, kindly regaled the history of the club at the town hall to the current players (those who were sober enough at the time), a few ex-players (those who could be bothered to turn up), some of the staff (those not fired/given up), and a handful of fans (the good guys) who had been invited.

Bernhard Halford was definitely there (always one for a party is Bernie), but as the centenary fell approximately seven weeks after Swales was ousted by Mr Chairman, Pete was probably at home still cleaning his suit trying to get that eggy smell out.

One hundred years and we get bloody Mayoress Sheila Smith. Can't wait for the next one.

---

1 Yes, I know I already mentioned this, but we were so crap that you have to forgive me for clinging on to anything that doesn't make me break down and cry.
2 Pah – what does he know?
3 Badoom, tish!
4 I think he was getting a tad excited about the 'age of £3 million players' a little too early.
5 The enemy of my enemy is my enemy ... or my frenemy ... enemy friendly? ... friendly enemy? Let me get back to you on that one.
6 Hmm ... something about that doesn't bode well.
7 And you all thought he was obsessed.
8 Whoa there cowboy! Don't celebrate just yet.
9 Told you.
10 Actually, now that I think about it, this explains how shit things became, arf.
11 Couldn't be so that he wouldn't have to spend any of the money that he didn't have because Swales had blown it, could it? Nah...
12 Maybe he meant United fans.
13 That's the last time we'll ever see an Arab be interested in City.
14 I'm not telling you the time of KO, you can do your own damn research.
15 This includes the one-off Manchester City *v*. Hyde United game of 1934, where the winner would get to keep Wanda for Wednesday evenings. Don't worry; we won.
16 Or down, which we had done so much we were positively expert at it, but we really needed to start broadening our horizons and learn something new.
17 Who says it doesn't pay to be crap?

THE END OF AN ERA

Contrary to what millions were repeatedly saying all across the planet, the world did not end on 31 December, and with that non-event, the twenty-first century arrived.[1] City would, umm ... well, keep doing what they did best, which was not very much. After the miracle of 1999, City went on to prove that they were still on the ascendancy by scoring 485 goals in Division One under the tutorship of Joe Royle, with Shaun Goater scoring ninety-two of them during a game at Stockport in December.

The plan was to push on straight back into the Premiership, after all we were founding members and the other teams were completely lost without us. The plan was expertly executed, and City found themselves among old friends once more for the start of the 2000/01 season, after finishing second in the League. However, it was deemed by David Bernstein that Joe Royle had not fully understood the whole plan, when, at the end of that season, City found themselves returning to Division One. Up stepped Kevin Keegan to introduce his own blend of football, which completely did away with any kind of defence, or indeed a goalkeeper for that matter. Although fans were a little concerned, they soon came to love the weekly scorelines of 37-29 and took Keegan in as one of their own.

So successful was Keegan's style of play, that the FA awarded City an extra three points, 'just for the sheer hell of it'.

You know how TV spells out numbers if the scoreline looks like a misprint? Sky Sports spent 4 per cent of their budget on City results that season.

Pos	Club	Pld	W	D	L	GF	GA	GD	Pts
1	Manchester City	46	31	6	9	2,483	1,914	569	99

However, there was much sorrow on the horizon. The 2002/03 season was to be City's very last at Maine Road, and the reason for this could be traced to way back in 1994, when the city of Manchester attempted to win the bid to host the Olympics. Of course once the IOC had stopped laughing and realized that they were actually being serious, they suggested that perhaps the Olympics was a little too big for the city and maybe they should start somewhere a little smaller by hosting something that no one had ever heard of, or indeed was interested in.

And so, in 2002, the city of Manchester hosted the Commonwealth Games,[2] but this was only possible if someone was to make use of the £112 million stadium after the 'totally worth it in the financial sense of the word' four weeks of usage. Up stepped City, who had been looking at improving Maine Road (I use the word 'improving' much like a doctor would want to 'improve' a dead person's condition), but then got wind of someone, for all intents and purposes, giving away a brand new stadium for free.

Of course, if City had not won at Wembley in 1999 against Gillingham it all might not have happened, because as happy as the City of Manchester was to give a brand new stadium away they weren't stupid enough to give it to a third tier side.

On 11 May 2003, City played – and naturally lost – their very last ever game at Maine Road. While many knew that City could neither turn down the offer, or waste yet more money on what was once the Wembley of the North, the goodbyes were still hard to swallow. There was an auction of basically everything of the stadium afterwards, but due to the locals nicking anything that wasn't nailed down beforehand, it didn't quite raise as much money as was hoped.

So it was that City found themselves a new home, which was totally befitting of their Premiership status, and of course with a dedicated and never-give-up guy at the helm, City were going to conquer all before them.[3]

However, you remember all those big buys from the 1910s, 1930s, 1950s ... actually, forget that, do you just remember them? City did it again in 2003, in the shape of £4 million defender Sylvain Distin –at that time, he was the club's most expensive defender ever. This time, though, Distin proved to be worth every penny and was named the Player of the Year in his first season. In the following season he was named captain and even popped up with a couple of goals. But with City every silver lining has its cloud, and he left in 2007. For free. To bloody Portsmouth! For free!

Anyway, other than a couple of squeaky-bum moments, City faired okay back in the Premiership (or as it was soon to be called, the Premier League, essentially because everyone outside of the UK had always known it as such), even when finishing sixteenth at the end of the 2003/04 season; a brand new sponsor in First Advice certainly helped. The company helped even further by giving City all the money upfront before the financial service company collapsed and went into receivership, meaning City were wearing the name of a business that no longer existed. We're not really here.

Trouble was more problems were about to befall City and this was partly due to being unable to balance the chequebook (or completely ignoring it, and doing whatever the hell they wanted – you take your pick). What also didn't help was that Mr Reliable, Kevin Keegan, woke up one morning in 2005 and decided that he never wanted to return to work ever again. 'Finished with football management,' he declared, 'I'm never doing it again.'[4]

Before he did resign, however, he had been pushing Bernstein to invest heavily in players, while Bernstein, who had been down that road once already, refused to do so. However, instead of sticking to his guns as chairman, he upped and left. This allowed Keegan to run to the new men in charge, John Wardle and David Makin, who, with just under 30 per cent of the shares, owned more than anyone else did. While this may sound impressive, the share ownership of the club was so fractured you could have driven a dump-truck through and no one would have noticed. Even Mr Chairman still owned shares and had a seat on the board, though he was never to be seen again or ever make use of said seat.

To be fair to the City-supporting Mr Wardle, an incredibly wealthy man, he put his own money where his mouth was. To be unfair to Mr Wardle, Keegan did one, not long after. Cheers, Kev.

Wardle, in fact, continued to pile money into the club, but no matter how much came in, more was going out. These things don't happen overnight, people! And it can be traced all the way back to 1973, when Peter Swa ... no, I'm not going into that again, I refuse to, now where the hell did I put my Prozac. Once Kev had done one, the board, realizing they had no manager (losing to Spurs 2-1 in the process), turned to Mr Relaxed and Calm – Stuart Pearce.

Pearce initially didn't do too badly, winning four, drawing four and losing one of the nine games left in the season. Trouble was, one of those draws, the last game of the season against Middlesbrough, needed to be a win to get City into the UEFA Cup. So when you have a £5 million striker sat on the bench with 2 minutes plus 5 stoppage minutes, what do you do? Exactly! You replace Claudio Reyner for Nicky Weaver, who then swaps with David James and runs up the pitch with all the finesse and grace of a blind hippo. Strangely, it almost worked and, had Fowler not had his penalty saved, City would have been in Europe the following season. So (almost) successful was this crazy idea that Pearce did it again when he was in charge of the England U21s, by throwing on the Peterborough 'keeper, Joe Lewis, with 15 minutes left on the clock. England won the game 7-0, with a young Joe Hart looking on incredulously from the goal line.

Unfortunately, City began to slowly regress, not just on the field, but off it, too. At the end of the 2005/06 season, City's revenues were the seventeenth highest in the world, although much of this could be attributed to Ian Wright suggesting his step-son should be playing much, much more and at a better team. That went well, didn't it, Ian? The 2006/07 season saw City break yet another record – scoring ten goals at home all season – and if that wasn't bad enough did not score at all at home after New Year's Day. 'Manchester City 0' was the first thing usually written by journalists as a match report *prior* to kick-off.

While Pearce was apparently not the one to serve the fans attractive football, he did at least stick to his old-fashioned footballing roots, when Bernado Corradi was sent off against Manchester United for receiving two yellow cards, one of which was for diving. Pearce promised he was not going to accept any bullshit from his players and that Corradi would never dive again particularly once he'd had a 'word' with him. Essentially, this meant Pearce was going to go all sergeant on his arse and shout at him so loudly that Corradi would have shat himself before having what little shit remained being beaten out of him.

At the beginning of the 2006/07 season, Manchester City became the first professional football club to sign up with Stonewall, an organisation that helps to promote gay, lesbian and bisexual equality in the workplace – that'll explain the 'love bites' thing at the end of the 2011/12 season.

Wardle, as rich as he was, simply could not afford to keep spending his own money to keep the club going, and realized something had to be done – find a new owner.[5] The club was going down faster than a two-bit hooker and so they quietly started the search for someone with more cash than sense, after the shareholders had agreed that they would sell should the right man turn up. Perhaps this is the reason why Pearce could not offer Pep Guardiola an eighteen-month contract when he arrived for a ten-day trial in August 2005. Never mind, huh? It was not like that fella was ever going to amount to anything anyway…

Former City defender Ray Ranson, who had started his career at the club in 1976 and stayed for eight years, had amassed a small fortune with various business dealings after he had hung up his boots for good. He was very much interested in taking over at the club and promised to pay off all the loans, buy everyone out, and inject a hefty sum to get things moving again. Ex-Blue, with cash, and investors behind him. Sounds awesome, yes?

Sadly, no. He had attempted to buy Aston Villa – twice – but failed, and Wardle and Makin were not entirely sure he could come up with the proposed £90 million he was offering. Of course there was also the little matter of Leeds United financially imploding apparently due, in part, to massively expensive loan deals set up by Ranson. Perhaps City were doing the right thing for once?

Eventually City saw the 'right man' step forward – international, all-round nice guy, and in no way in trouble with the authorities, former Thai PM Thaksin Shinawatra. He had already been on the hunt for a Premier League club, having looked at Fulham FC and, as a self-confessed Liverpool fan, obviously Liverpool FC too, even going so far as making an unsuccessful bid for them. Trouble was it had been said that he didn't have a clue about 'football the game', let alone football as ownership, and possibly no clue about City fans' sense of loyalty. After being snapped with Alex Ferguson in 2001 in Thailand, he handed him his own personal United shirt (No. 52, if you're interested, it was his fifty-second birthday after all, bless). But, granted access to the club's accounts (first time for everything, I guess), he was immediately interested in stumping up a large amount of cash and taking control.

However, as this is Manchester City, things didn't quite go smoothly. Thailand, which was now in control by the country's military, charged Shinawatra with corruption, seized over £800 million of his money and placed his wife under arrest.[6]

But this didn't stop the takeover; we were desperate, remember? Or at least the board was desperate. No, everybody was desperate. On 6 July 2007, he took control after handing over £81 million to gain 75 per cent of the shares. Fit and proper person's test? He looks healthy enough to me.

Good friends Shinawatra was with Sven Göran Eriksson, he of ex-England and loving-the-ladies fame, and promptly put him in charge of the squad, getting rid of Pearce in the process – City were going to rule with an iron fist under the SS. This was City's first ever foreign manager – that is if you discount the previous eight Scottish ones, although to be fair to City, taking the Scots-route hadn't been too bad down the years, that is until we hit the triple-headed monster that was Benson, McNeill, and Frizzell.

The media went into its usual frenzy and City found themselves front and centre, with the fans hoping and praying (and offering their firstborns) that the nightmare they had been forced to endure for the last thirty years was finally over. Had the fans realized that Thaksin was under the impression that City hammering United twice a year was perfectly normal, they may have paused for thought.

At first, it did seem like the nightmare was over. SGE's first season in charge saw City do the double over Manchester United and amass their best points tally in the Premier League. By November, City were third. Yes, third. Somehow, Frank and Sven were bringing football back to Maine ... the other place, and the City faithful were loving it (we will ignore and forget the 6-0 drubbing at Chelsea). However, it could and should have been better, as the first half of the season was as brilliant as the second half was diabolical; an Everton in reverse if you will (season 2012/13 notwithstanding).

It didn't happen overnight of course, just a slow drip, drip, of not quite doing enough before a total and utter collapse. Superman pants indeed...

Friend or no friend, Thaksin went on record as saying SGE was out at the end of the season, even though City had managed to worm their way into the UEFA Cup under the 'fair play' rules – this was primarily because the new owners considered everyone replaceable, from those at the very top to those all the way down at the very bottom, like the shoeshine boys. 'We got three-year-olds who could feed their families for a whole year on what you get paid in one week – oh, and we don't see enough hermaphrodites on the payroll.'

People in Thailand simply shrugged their shoulders, muttering things like 'Well, what did you expect? Just be thankful he's not been shot.' Oh, those Thais and their wicked sense of humour.

The fans who actually liked SGE were horrified, and started an SOS protest, with even the team suggesting that they would go on strike.[7] Sven, to his credit, pleaded with the team not to do this and, after considering all possibilities, decided he was right and stepped out onto the pitch against Middlesbrough for the last game of the season. Who can really say what the score would have been if the players had actually not tried.

Gary says: 'Hey! I was here then. There I was hard at work bringing in the likes of Mark, and Jô ... and Wayne Bridge ... and that Ben Tal-Haim fella. 'Oh, thems were the days.'

There had been some talk from Frank that he wanted José Mourinho in the hotseat prior to giving SGE the boot. Frank didn't appreciate Sven's strong attitude, so quite how he would have handled the sheepskin-coat wearer, is anyone's guess.

Outside of football, things were getting worse and worse for our owner; on 31 July 2008, his wife was convicted and sentenced to three years in jail and both were explicitly told to stay put while the authorities sorted things out, which of course they did do. In Beijing. And then in England. And later on in Dubai.

However, two days after Sven left, in came Mark Hughes, who had turned down Chelsea to come to the City of Manchester Stadium. The fans were becoming very unsure about the future of their club and were not overly enthusiastic about having an ex-United player in charge, but precisely eighty-nine days later things were about to get very, very silly indeed.

Happy Birthday Manchester City!
16 April

1-0 *v.* Liverpool
2-1 *v.* Hamburg
So the Germans have forgiven us after all.

Notable Players of the 2000s

George Weah, 1 August 2000–16 October 2000

After winning more player of the year awards than you could shake a player of the year award at Weah, quite unbelievably, joined Joe Royle's City just as they re-entered the Premier League for a staggering £30,000 a week. Weah grew up in war-torn Liberia, had been through some terrible shit in his life, so quite what Royle did to him forcing him to tear up his own contract is unknown. Saying that, he wasn't actually that good any more.

Vicente Matías Vuoso, 2002–03

Throughout their history Manchester City have had a fair few Argentinian players and they have worked out due to their work ethic. So when Keegan paid £3.5 million for Vuoso in June of 2002 for a striker who had been paired up with Diego Forlan at Independiente, it seemed like a bargain. He got no goals. No starts. No substitutions. Nothing. Absolutely, nothing. No, wait. He got the No. 21 shirt. Fantastic.

Nicolas Anelka, 2002–05

It was purely a matter of time before Anelka arrived. Not because we were in desperate need of a striker of his quality (although we were), but that we were thankfully next on his 'clubs to play for' list. He can currently be found working his way through the clubs of the Football Conference division.

Sun Jihai, 2002–08

In 2002, Manchester City added over 1 billion fans to its fanbase when they signed the Chinese footballer Jihai. Sven Göran Erikson did not understand this and dropped him when he became manager, promptly upsetting a sixth of the world's population.

Árni Gautur Arason, 2003–04

This Icelandic 'keeper only made two appearances for City, but it was his first against Tottenham Hotspur that will live on in City folklore.

After Barton had been sent off (because that's what he does), City were down 3-0 at half-time. Arason then double saved – at opposite corners of his net – and City ended up uncharacteristically winning 4-3 in what has been described as one of the greatest FA Cup comebacks of all time. Gordon Banks *v*. Pele ... meh.

Claudio Reyna, 2003–07

American soccer player of the century – no, seriously – arrived from Sunderland for around £1.5 million. He fared okay but was hindered by injuries during his four seasons with us. Why is he worthy of a mention? Because now that City are famous and stuff, American networks were legally obliged to mention Reyna on all City matches shown, which in turn means America loves us. Hi, America. Oh, there's also that NYCFC thing.

Micah Richards, 2005–14

You know when it feels like something is just 'part of the furniture'? That's Richards, that was. Only he was 'really good furniture'. He once lost his temper so badly after being subbed that Paul Dickov had to calm him down. Paul Dickov!

Joe Hart, 2006–Present

Purchased in 2006 for £42.06 (new money), he is now reputed to be worth so much that it would be cheaper to buy Belgium.

Kiatprawut Saiwaeo, 2007–08

Saiwaeo was one of three Taiwanese footballers (the other two being the somewhat more pronounceable, Suree Sukha and Teerasil Dangda) brought over by Thaksin to be given season-long trials, irrespective of the fact that none of them would have been given a working permit. As soon as Thaksin went, so did they.

Omar Elabdellaoui, 2008–13

It was officially said that Elabdellaoui had a big future at City and was justly rewarded with a first-team number and named in City's Europa squad of 2009/10. He sat on the bench once. Massive.

Vincent Kompany, 2008–Present
About eight days before the money arrived, Kompany appeared for a rumoured £6 million from Hamburger SV – proving that even Hughes could get the odd thing correct, even if he had him initially playing in the wrong position…

Pablo Zabaleta, 2008–Present
'I'll play anywhere where the boss tells me to play; if he wants me in goal, I'll ask where the gloves are,' the Zab-Man once famously said, just before donning the Moonchester costume, and serving some fries. He also bleeds blue blood, and literally scores once every blue moon.

A Manchester City Fan of the 2000s Has His Say

Name: Dean Philips
Age: 27
First City game ever attended: I forget which, but it was a cup game in 2002.

Why did I start following them? Dunno, really. Everyone's second favourite club, yeah? Well, unless you're a United fan, of course.

Least offensive club in the country, I reckon. Thing is though, them United fans constantly taking the piss, but are so ecstatic when they beat us in the derby, or are livid when we beat them. If we don't matter, why does it bother them so much? Liverpool, biggest rivals my arse they are, or at least to the fans at any rate.

That's why I didn't join up with them, y'see; arrogance, don't like it. Quite happy being mediocre, although the stadium's nice, ain't it? Not sure what we're supposed to call it though – Eastlands? City of Manchester Stadium? Everyone still says Maine Road, though, but what's it matter what it's called? At least it ain't The Eidos Stadium! That would just sound silly.

Hopes? I'd like to think we could get a trophy in one of the cups, one day the League Cup would probably be easier, 'cause no one cares about it.

Stuart Pearce? The passion is there, but not so sure about his tactics, but who could replace him? Got no money, have we? And probably never will.

---

1 Yes, I understand that the new millennium didn't actually start until 1 January 2001, but as everyone was so keen to throw the world's biggest party, nobody cares what you think.
2 The Commonwealth essentially consists of countries England had once invaded, and are still too crap and limp-wristed to do anything about it.
3 Now if they can just hold on to it for longer than 5 minutes.
4 For further information as to never doing it again, please see BBC's *Superstars* 1976, Poodle-perm 1980, releasing a crap single 1980, Newcastle 1997, Fulham 1999, England 2000, Newcastle (again) 2008 and speeding conviction 2009.
5 C'mon, nobody is that rich.
6 Don't you just hate it when that happens? The money bit, I mean, not the wife bit.
7 'Save Our Sven', in case you didn't know – not likely to have been 'Start Of Shit', was it?

THE MANCHESTER DHABI

Manchester City had been in existence, in one form or another, since 1880; born of an idea of a poor Irish woman (alright! maybe! yeesh, you people!). The club had seen many ups and downs[1] and the fans had been privileged to witness many firsts in the English game of football.[2]

However, on the final day of August 2008 – 46,677 days after Ardwick's very first game played – something quite extraordinary occurred – Manchester City was turned into an actual business (still a sodding football club though – yeah I'm talking to you Edwards). The Abu Dhabi United Group quietly turned up at the door and deposited £200 million into the mailbox, and after explaining that the money had been found down the side of some old sofa, and that there was 'plenty more where that came from', they brought forth another shock to the suffering City fans.

On the final day of the summer transfer window, they brought Robinho de Souza to the club for a British record transfer fee. All of this, to the supporters, was akin to being told that a naked Angelina Jolie was waiting for you in the bedroom, only to discover upon opening the door that she had brought her unknown to the world twin sister, too.

But how did all of this come about? Please, gather round, and pull up a chair.

Thaksin Shinawatra had moved heaven and earth to get his frozen assets back but was getting nowhere, particularly seeing as though he was now being tried in Thailand in his absence, as his wife had been. This posed a tiny little problem with the Premier League, who forbade anyone convicted of corruption to control a club. On top of this, Shinawatra needed to get his hands on some cold, hard cash.[3] So, too, did Manchester City, because they basically didn't have any due to Frank charging City interest on all the players he had been buying for the club, which was incredibly nice of him. City had to go running off to Wardle for the umpteenth time to ask for a few quid to pay for stuff like wages, and bills, and everything. Obviously this made his day complete.

As if that wasn't enough, Frank and his wife were quickly running out of safe countries to go to, but, as is always the case, it's not what you know, but who you know. Enter stage-left, Dr Sulaiman Al-Fahim.

Sulaiman (so the world thought at the time) was an incredibly wealthy guy; the only trouble was, he had no access to the aforementioned sofa and was merely a face to put out there for the benefit of the media, or, as some might say, a 'hanger on'.[4] Indeed, the doctor was a hanger on, and was soon turfed out on his ear, after stating that Manchester City would buy Christiano Ronaldo for £134 million, knock down Old Trafford and build a training facility on the moon to acclimatise players to 'high-altitude matches'. He was later found hanging around Portsmouth FC wearing a black cape and holding a giant sickle.

To say that the world's press went all a tad nuts would be the understatement of the century and when it emerged that the real guy in charge of ADUG was His Royal Highness, Sheikh Mansour bin Zayed Al Nahyan, and that they had a net worth of $1 trillion, journalists began to dribble on themselves (more so than normal) and began writing articles with colourful graphics about how many Big Macs Manchester City could now afford to buy.

Of course, ADUG couldn't understand what all the fuss was about, as we were only talking £200 million with an investment of around another £1 billion or so in the years to come. 'Did you not see the sofa?' asked one ADUG official, 'I dunno. You spend a billion or so and white people lose it.'

The blue half of Manchester wept with joy, knowing that the club's new owners seriously meant business, and finally the sleeping (while having nightmares) giant would soon be awoken.

The red half of Singapore – sorry – Greater Manchester, pointed jealous fingers at the blue half, saying that 'you can't buy history and success'; in spite of the fact that Manchester United had spent £104 million on Veron, Nistleroy, Rooney and Ferdinand before the supposed mega bucks arrived in the form of their new owners, the Glazers. Additionally, it is physically impossible to 'buy' history. They never were very smart.

Anyway, the 2008/09 season got properly under way (once everyone had calmed down a little) and great things were expected of Manchester City and their record signing – Robinho. However, come the end of the season, those great expectations had seemingly fallen flat on their face, as the club finished tenth and Robinho was discovered to have severe allergies to rain, playing away from home, and being looked at funny. Despite this, he finished as the club's top scorer with fifteen. Mind you, a further eighteen other City players also scored in the League that season, breaking the Premier League record for the number of different scorers from one club in one season, with no less than twelve players finding the back of the net on a single occasion. Even £19 million Jô got in on the act against Portsmouth, which was a very important goal to be fair, as beating them 5-0 would have been unacceptable. Although like the rumoured Kinkladze deal in the previous decade, his fee, in July, was allegedly inflated to the tune of £13 million by Frank so that it looked like he was spending massive money. Although, even at £6 million, our owner was robbed blind.

While those nineteen different scorers was very special, City had had nineteen different scorers in one season twice before, in 1893/94 (although technically speaking that was Ardwick), and in 1997/98 (but that was in Division One, the season City were relegated to Division Two).

However, while Mark Hughes had not been appointed by ADUG they insisted that he stayed on at the helm, even though many were calling for his head (and in some cases, quite literally, too).

Manchester City haters, which for some reason had slowly grown in number since August of 2008 from an all-time high of seventeen in 1973, began to laugh at the club. 'All that money and you still can't get it right?'

Little did the haters know that this was exactly what ADUG had planned, for it had already worked wonders in the 1960s under Joe Mercer; mediocrity in the first season (we did have Mark Hughes at the helm, after all), followed by a trophy and Champion's League football, followed by the Premier League title. Don't you just love it when a plan comes together?[5]

Hughes obviously knew a lot about City's rich history and showed it by attempting to bring in the modern-day Fred Tilson in the shape of Roque Santa Cruz. Trouble was, Cruz was under the impression that Tilson never played football. Ever.

The 2009/10 season started off well, with the first four games ending in wins. Next up, derby day. There must have been a massive solar flare hitting the planet Earth that day, as the laws of time and physics were inexplicably altered after Manchester United scored the winner in the 174th minute of injury time. Alex Ferguson celebrated like he had never celebrated in his life, pausing for a moment to face a TV camera and calmly explain that 'it's just a mere game, and three points at the end of the day,' before galloping off across the turf like someone who had just won the European lottery jackpot.

Mark Hughes was rather annoyed, yet determined that this result would not put a dampener on the season. So annoyed was he, that he got the team to produce seven draws on the trot.

During December of that year, City travelled to White Hart Lane, and the only person in the stadium that day who did not know Hughes was out on his ear, seemed Hughes himself. In fact all he had to do was pick up a copy of the matchday Spurs programme, and see an article written by Roberto Mancini outlining his thoughts for the game and his hopes for the season. Later that week, Hughes was on a Caribbean beach consoling himself with his multi-million pound severance cheque.

2009 was also the year that one Carlos Tevez arrived under much fanfare. He had been at Manchester United, where the fans had been screaming for Ferguson to sign him only to say he was 'crap anyway' when City signed him. No one paid any attention to the fact that Tevez had previously pledged his allegiance to Manchester United (then walked), West Ham (then walked), Corinthians (then walked), Boca Juniors (then ... well, you get the idea). But we are City (super City, no less), so everything's good.

Anyway, Roberto Mancini arrived and by the end of the season City finished in fifth place, guaranteeing them the much sought after Thursday night football that the club had been craving for.

Remembering that the new owners had a few pennies rolling around, during the summer off-season, City spent what was described in the *Business Times* as 'a shitload' on several new players. Chairmen of the major European clubs began to complain that Manchester City were being unfair, but then smiled to themselves as they remembered that the Financial Fair Play rules that were to come into effect would see the club being laughed at by all.[6]

However, all were still thinking 'old City', not this new and improved beast. After all, you don't spend all that money without a plan, do you?[7] 'Think of a number,' said Etihad, the Abu Dhabi airline, when they approached ADUG on the subject of club sponsorship, 'then add a few noughts. But we do insist that 12 per cent of all goal celebrations are done doing the airplane; although doing that lips-spluttering thing is optional.'

Manchester City Hide United

In 1885, Hyde Football Club was formed and then reformed after the First World War as Hyde United, and yes, the colour red was predominant throughout the club and the stadium – that was until Manchester City knocked on their door, asking if the reserves could play there.

Manchester City effectively sponsored the club, re-laid the pitch and painted the entire stadium blue. As a thank you, Hyde officially and permanently dropped the 'United' part, changed their kit to blue and white for one season and changed their crest to blue.

That's one United down, just several more to go.

The 2010/11 season was the one where everyone sat up and noticed; Manchester City won something.[8] 1976 was the last time the club had managed to get their grubby hands on some silver (and even that was the poor man's cup, the League Cup, which mattered to absolutely no one save for the winners themselves), but all that changed on 16 May, after beating Stoke at Wembley to get the FA Cup.

What this also did was to upset Manchester United fans due to them so lovingly tending to a banner at Old Trafford, which was updated every year letting us know how long it had been since winning something. Because a long time-span can make one forgetful, the author thanks them for keeping him informed, although regretfully they have now stopped doing so for some reason, which is a shame. Even though we went to a great deal of trouble and made them a new one starting again at '00' years.

Manchester City also finished in third place, level on points with Chelsea but with an inferior goal difference – how horrible is that? To know you could have placed higher if you'd only scored more, or let in less? Ask Leeds United fans how they felt when Manchester United did the same thing to them to win the League title in 1965.

What this also meant, of course, was that Manchester City were now dining at the Champion's League table. Cream of chicken soup, please. However, no one could have foreseen what was to happen, for the curse of Munich was to strike at a Manchester club once more.

You would think that, when you earn a gazillion pounds a week, if you are told to enter the field of play singing the "Star-Spangled Banner 'dressed in nothing but a carrier bag, you would do. Apparently not so in the case of one Mr Carlos Tevez. After a Mancunian fatwa had been put in place, he instantly did one to Argentina, only to return when it had been removed.

This could have derailed City's entire season, but once again, in an untypical City manner, the team did even better, only to collapse once he came back. He wasn't playing of course, but when he did return to the field of play, City ironically played better. I think I just confused everyone there.

January 2011 saw City claim yet another first, when both Yaya and Kolo Toure scored in the same game in the 4-3 win against

Wolverhampton Wanderers.[9] Brothers had often played together and on occasion had both scored, too, but this was the first time in the Premier League, so obviously the countless times it had happened before didn't count for anything.

The George Town Derby

1949 was the last time there had been a true Manchester derby day (thanks, for that, Mr Hitler). Anything after that, or even before, were two teams from two different boroughs playing against each other.

In 2012, 'Man U' went one stage further. The club effectively became a Cayman Islands company by moving the club's registration to the tax-free Caribbean haven. Removing the word 'Manchester' from its name, and now removing Greater Manchester entirely; give it fifty years and they'll probably be operating from the lunar surface and be known as Moonchester. 'It's dey Mancheester Derbee, and it's gunna bee fine. Yeah, man.'

Towards the close of the 2011/12 season, Manchester City found themselves back in the No.1 spot, after what could only be described as Manchester United 'bottling it'. This was due to the derby game at the Etihad, which had been named as 'the world's biggest ever thing that has ever happened since time began ever™'. Alex 'I don't play for a draw', Ferguson, turned up with a goalkeeper, eight defenders and two holding midfielders, and then got upset when City won the game 1-0.

At the end of United's final home game he told the Old Trafford faithful (well, the one's who hadn't already gone home before the final whistle), to get ready for 'the biggest celebration of their lives'. He was to make mention that what City did to his new best pal, Mark Hughes, was horrible and akin to kicking a puppy, and Hughes would be ready and wanting to pounce on his old employers when he was to take QPR to the Etihad on the last day of the season. And pounce they did, going into a 2-1 lead even though down to ten men.[10]

But this is City we are talking about – a club so desperate to cling on to their roots – and what better way could there be than to go into extra time to do what no other club had ever done before in the Premier League, needing to score two goals in injury time to show the new influx of fans what supporting the club really meant?

Ferguson should have known better, too, as he tentatively stepped onto the turf of Sunderland's Stadium of Light waiting for the final whistle some 140 miles or so away, but ultimately ending up looking like a lost geriatric who couldn't remember where he lived any more.

Commentators all around the world did 'a Gary Neville' and made lots of uncomfortable sex noises as Agüero slammed the ball into the QPR net, with City's fourty-fourth shot of the game, and with barely 90 seconds left on the clock. City fans cried, Ferguson looked like he wanted to cry, Mancini ran onto the pitch, QPR fans cheered and Sunderland fans did the Poznan. Not too shabby for a day's work. Mind you, Ferguson couldn't be happy for us, and began muttering things like 'City only had to play against ten men and they got an extra 5 minutes,' because of course things like that had never happened for his team.

At the end of the 2011/12 season, Bobby had signed an extension to his contract, with a pay rise to boot. It was only natural that within weeks of the new season starting the media, as one, said he was going to be sacked. The main reason for this was that José Mourinho was bored at Real Madrid (nothing to do with Barcelona being seventy-four points in front – no, Sir), and that, in his own words, he would be coming to the Premier League the following season.

There was also the curious case of the summer transfer window. Before the media had started with their 'Mancini will be sacked' approach, they were going all 'Doctor' Sulaiman Al-Fahim on us, stating that every player with a price tag of at least £50 million hanging around their necks would be wearing blue shirts come opening day of the season; instead Maicon and a couple of others turned up.

The season of 2012/13 kicked off just like the previous one had ended, with City crowned Champions when they beat Chelsea at Wembley in the Community Shield. It was expected that they would be once again battling it out with Manchester United for the top spot – either that, or be so far ahead come the end of February that for the last ten games Mancini would field an entire team comprised of academy lads and three members of the public who had won an online prize draw on the official site.

Come February, however, while City were indeed firmly in one of the Champion's League places, they had seemingly forgotten how to score and allowed United to run off into the distance.

27 October saw Manchester City break yet another record when they played Swansea City at home. 12 minutes and 42 seconds of injury time was played at the end of the second half, far more than had ever been played before – that is unless you do not include Manchester United's injury time win over City in 2009/10.

City had previously been booted out of the League Cup by Villa. Yes, that Villa – Aston Villa. And, although expectations had been high for the Champion's League itself, City found themselves in the toughest group of all time, in what was essentially a Champion's of Champions Group, with two from that group reaching the semi-finals.

'Lowest ever total points accrued,' said the media. 'Ah, but,' said City, 'Villarreal didn't get any points last season in our group.' 'No, lowest by an English side,' added the media. 'Oh.'

As it turned out, it wasn't a particularly good year for any English side, as Chelsea, the Champion's League holders, were dumped out of the Europa League, Arsenal got spanked by the Germans and United, thinking they had a chance, were beaten by the Spanish (or the referee, depending upon your point of view).

There was the FA Cup though and Rafa Benitez wanted it badly. Once City had quietly explained he couldn't have it, the Blues moved on to Wembley to take on the mighty Wigan Athletic, knowing full well that anyone from the North West of England attending that match by train would be stuck in the capital overnight.[11] Because, of course, no one would ever want to go to Manchester from London on a Saturday night.[12]

86,254 people turned up to watch what was evidently going to be a walk in the park for the former English Champions. Of those 86,254, according to who you believe, as many as a record 60,000

Blues turned up because, apparently, Wigan fans didn't want their tickets. What that essentially meant was that Manchester City broke their own record as most supported club ever at a competitive match played at Wembley, although this was now the 'new' Wembley. Manchester City ... continually breaking records, good or bad.

As Wigan was the only team actually playing, come full time, Wigan won and left Manchester City without a pot to piss in.[13] City fans still congratulated Wigan and the fans though, because: 'Nah, mate, we ain't arrogant; we know we were shit.'

As it transpired, City winning the Premier League in 2012 staved off 650 million United fans' tears for another twelve months.[14] Alex Ferguson, unbeknown to anyone, had decided he'd had enough and wanted to move to the more leisurely and laid-back boardroom, and had every intention of doing so until that 'Agüeroooooo' moment scuppered the idea. Did we get any thanks for it though? Pft.

Incidentally, the moment Ferguson announced his retirement in what was actually the real 'the biggest celebration of our lives', all hell broke loose over at Old Trafford; shares plunged 5 per cent, major trophy winner David Moyes turned up, Wayne Rooney handed in a(nother) transfer request, Arsenal fans realised Ferguson had essentially done them just so that the Scotsman could win a final title, boardroom managers up and down the country wondered if they would need a new manager next week, and City fans just sat back and laughed. It was a rather good couple of days, which were extended a little further as the footballing gods were angered by United's presence in Manchester. Heavy thunder and lightning filled the skies and the city was deluged with hail and rain coming from thick, black clouds, as they paraded the Premier League trophy around. Not that a bit of water should bother some plastics.

Happy Birthday Manchester City!
16 April

1-0 *v.* Manchester United
HA!

Those good couple of days didn't last for very long though, as, just prior to City's trip to Wembley, reports were surfacing from Spain that (once again) Mancini was out on his ear, and this time he was to be replaced by Malaga's young and sprightly, Manuel Pellegrini. The fact that these reports were based upon the good ol' 'Dr' Sulaiman Al-Fahim was neither here nor there. Trouble was the City hierarchy were as silent as a very silent thing, and refused point-blank to say anything on the subject one way or the other. Until they did.

Exactly 1 year, 4 hours and 39 minutes after Sergio Agüero put the ball in the back of the net against QPR, Roberto 'I don't like purple' Mancini was relieved of his duties as manager. Manchester City, a club now known throughout the world, went into the final two games of the season sans (proper) manager. Brian Kidd stepped up to the plate and won the first match, which meant he had a chance to become the first ever City manager with a 100 per cent win record; bloody Norwich ruining it for everyone (again).

The 2013/14 season would see City with a fresh start, and in fact every club in the Premier League saw it as that now that Alex Ferguson had retired from management.

The 'Engineer's' job (when he eventually arrived, as City had already completed a mini-tournament in the USA) was five trophies in five years and come January of his first season, the press began to get all giddy at the prospect of Manchester City completing the quadruple. Naturally, City fans laughed at this explaining that 'one or possibly two will do just fine thank you very much'.

What had been called for longer than anyone could remember, the 'Big Top Four' of the Premier League was now called a rather ludicrous 'Top Seven'; this may have been not to rub it too much into the faces of Manchester United fans, so that was a nice touch.

However, while City were competing on all four fronts they were also looking to break goalscoring records, utilizing what was being referred to as 'the Kevin Keegan method but with the addition of a defensive line'. Arsenal had managed to score three but were still hammered, Bayern scored two in the first 12 minutes at home and lost (winning 2-0 and losing for the first time in almost thirty-eight years), Manchester United were convincingly outplayed in both derbies, and when other teams didn't want to score City decided to just score a bucketload themselves. It didn't take them long to break a record that had stood since the 1956/57 season – most goals scored in all competitions. Manchester United had held it with a total of 143 – MUFC breaking records and losing others in the space of ten months. Not in my lifetime? HA!

There were still some fans who wanted Mancini back early on in the season, and while that view stopped at the end of the footballing calender, they still were very appreciative of what Bobby Manc had done, so raised several thousand pounds for a full-page 'thank you' in the Italian *Gazzetta dello Sport* newspaper thanking him. No one had any idea if he even read the damn thing, but he must have at least got wind of it when he reciprocated with his own 'thank you', which must have cost all of £27.54.

Sunday 2 March 2014 presented Pellegrini with the opportunity of gaining City's first trophy as they toddled back down to the capital and on to Wembley to take on the might of Sunderland. The Engineer took two City squads with him that day, using the not so good eleven in the first half and the infinitely better eleven in the second half. Thankfully, the referee didn't notice the change and City lifted their first trophy of the season.

Of course, things weren't all warm and cuddly, as fighting on all four fronts had allowed Liverpool to get their act together (play the City way basically) and overtake them. It was certainly going to be an exciting finish to the Premier League.

Sadly, however, all good things must come to an end, and on 22 April 2014, they very much did and David Moyes was fired. After months and months of hilarity, watching records being broken left, right, and centre, the laughter stopped. There was much wailing and gnashing of teeth across all social media, as the Chosen One was sent packing.[15] Norwich's chance of pulling off an unlikely win versus United ended abruptly.

Outside of the Premier League battle that was turning into a wonderful threesome (but the sort without the strawberry flavoured lube), Manchester City were busy spreading their tentacles across the globe. There were some City fans who merely shrugged their shoulders and turned their attention to other things, as these two clubs were not really going to be Manchester City juniors. Those, who did sit up and notice, however, realised what was going on – it was a money-making and City awareness scheme. It is highly unlikely that without UEFA introducing the Financial Fair Play Rules, the takeover of Melbourne Heart and the birth of New York City FC would ever have happened. Cheers, Michel Platini.

Other clubs had before looked at doing what City were doing; most notably, Barcelona, but nothing had ever come of it. Mind you, things are always easier when you have a spare quarter of a billion burning a hole in your pocket – you know that feeling, right?

At the beginning of June 2014, Melbourne Heart was renamed Melbourne City (possibly in an attempt to confuse everyone with the MCFC acronym), introduced a brand new badge (with two little, cute hearts on it – bless), relegated the home red-and-white kit to away matches and introduced City's Embassy Mild third kit for home games.

Not content with having two extra clubs, City also bought into the J-League club Yokohama F. Marinos. On top of that, it was said that clubs in South Africa, Argentina, and China would be created. It was obvious to all and sundry that City were intent on purchasing one club in every country on the planet, culminating in creating the Etihad World League.

Not content with all that contentment, City were soon to be opening a brand new academy campus where every level of the club would train and learn 'the City way', so that even eight-year-olds could be taught how to snatch defeat from out of the hands of victory.

Speaking of FFPR, at the end of April in 2014, City were found guilty of breaching the rules and given a punishment. No official word of what any of it was about came out because one of the rules stated that all findings were confidential and neither could anyone ask. No word of guilt or, otherwise, no word of punishment. It was all very Guantanamo Bay. This didn't stop the '£50 million fine' headlines though, or indeed stop Arsene Wenger from sticking his nose in and having a bit of a moan about spending too much money, just prior to signing his new £8 million a year contract.

As it turned out, the club were found to be guilty of having no debt and were handed a €60 million fine (with most of it to be returned) and a wage cap, which, as it turned out, was based upon amortisation and not all-in, so it essentially amounted to mean diddly squat. A reduced Champion's League squad meant that City only had to field five homegrown players and not the normal figure of seven, which is actually less of a percentage of the squad, and so, this too, amounted to diddly squat.

UEFA had obviously been reading 'The FA's Hate Campaign Against Manchester City' chapter in this book (sorry about that). Unknowledgeable fans lost their collective shit, but the club's right of reply basically read as one big 'up yours UEFA, we are City, Super City, and we'll do what we want', adding that the punishments weren't going to stop anything.

The end of the 2013/14 season came upon us, with Manchester City proudly sitting at the top requiring a draw to snatch the title. According to the media, it really should have gone second-place Liverpool, bascially because Luis Suarez hadn't bitten anyone for a while and their fans had been selling '2014 Champions' shirts for the last three months. But, after Liverpool figuratively and literally slipped, the title became City's to lose.

Fans hoping for a repeat of 2012 not to happen again all breathed a collective sigh of relief in the 49th minute when Kompany slotted the ball home from around 3 inches out to effectively seal the win and City's second title in three seasons. The fans, remembering the mass pitch invasion on 11 May 1968 to celebrate the title win, did so once more, exactly forty-six years later. Perhaps City fans do know their history.

Pellegrini had been given the instruction, as said earlier, to achieve five trophies in five years (the fact he had only been given a three-year contract to accomplish this fact was not questioned by anyone). Ten months into the job he'd already got two. It's a pity I can't cover the 2014/15 season, but this book has to stop somewhere.

---

1 Mostly downs.
2 Which as we all know by now, doesn't necessarily mean that was a good thing.
3 Even better when it's cold, hard and dirty.
4 Brad Pitt would probably have been a better face to choose. Hell, even The Face from *The A-Team* would have been more preferable (he's a City fan, y'know).
5 Told you, they should have got The Face.
6 In effect the FFP was brought in to stop clubs coming to eat at the top table, because naturally that would be unfair on those who were already at the table. No soup for you!
7 Well, to be fair, the pre-ADUG Manchester City actually did.
8 Message to my editor – this is not a typo.
9 It's okay, you can do the song, I can wait; you can carry on reading when you've finished.
10 The QPR players who featured that day were: Kenny, Hill, Taiwo, Ferdinand, Onuoha, Derry, Barton, Wright-Phillips, Mackie, Cisse, Zamora, Traore, and Bothroyd. I'll let you guess who was sent off.
11 Wembley is for finals and finals only. I don't care what the FA says.
12 Although I imagine there is plenty of demand for trains going from Manchester to London on a Saturday night after a football match *snigger*.
13 Yes, I know we had won the Community Shield at the beginning of that season, but how exactly does one piss 'in' a flat piece of metal?
14 What? That figure was in an official Manchester United press release.
15 The latter part not so much in the North East of England, arf.

CONCLUSION

It took an awfully long 48,028 days for the world to recognize that Manchester City were awesome. We had won things before – sometimes officially and wanted, and sometimes unofficially and unwanted – and we had moved home seven times. We enjoyed the good times and somehow managed to survive the bad times.

We have played against Bayern München and Real Madrid, Macclesfield Town and Gillingham, Liverpool Stanley and Halliwell (well, almost). We have played at home with attendance figures lower than 1,000 and as high as 84,569. We have had a gazillion managers; some have stayed for years, while others didn't even bother taking their coat off.

We have had great players (I've mentioned Colin Bell, yes?) and soul-destroying awful ones (take your pick). We have witnessed thrilling encounters, and life-sapping embarrassments with the opposition.

Opposition fans have at times cheered us, but have sometimes also laughed at us. We have had people try and tear City apart (occasionally by City themselves), and others who saw what we always had and tried their best to keep the club going. We have seen the worst of the worst and the best of the best.

But through it all, we, the fans, have always been there. It was, is, and forever more, will be in our blood. Family or fate brought us to the club (although recently it might simply be because we are, in the world's eyes, awesome), but we have never questioned it. So much of our lives is (unhealthily) devoted to Manchester City, causing those on the outside to wonder why. But maybe, just maybe, should they pick this book up (no, not this one, tell them to buy their own damn copy), they might understand.

CTWD

Notable Players of the ADUG Era

Frédéric Veseli, 2008–12
This promising Swiss centre-back came to the Elite Development squad from Lausanne-Sport, moving into the first team in 2010. Not one single appearance did Veseli make. Off to Manchester United he went and succeeded in no appearances there either. He signed a two-year deal at Ipswich Town in 2013, where, yes, he managed bugger all appearances there, too. Eat your heart out, James Cairns.

Jô, 2008–11
Awful. Simply awful. And that hair! What the hell is wrong with you?

Wayne Bridge, 2009–13
Word has it that Bridge was a footballer. Countless hours of research has yet to prove this as fact.

Nigel De Jong, 2009–12
The Chuck Norris of football; the man was an absolute beast in the City defence. The spirit of Mike Doyle fused with the Terminator. If the opposition didn't have Michael Biehn on their side they were seriously screwed.

Joleon Lescott, 2009–14
Stolen from Everton for a paltry £22 million (incurring the wrath of David Moyes because City were being 'cheap'), whenever Lescott played at home in the League, City never lost a match. Ever. Until we did.

Giselle Tavarelli, 2009–13

All-round professional good-looking person, Giselle, could, on occasion, take City fans' minds off the fact that we had for some inexplicable reason signed her husband, Roque Santa Cruz.

Aleksander Kolarov, 2010–Present

Cauliflower knows only one way to shoot on goal – hit it as hard as is (in)humanely possible. That and usually missing by a mile and a half. So, that's two ways … OK, Cauliflower knows only two ways to shoot …

David Silva, 2010–Present

What this man can do with a football just ain't normal. Of course, this means bloody awesome.

Yaya Touré, 2010–Present

City's very own X-man, once this juggernaut starts running, nothing on this Earth can stop him – except maybe his own 3-ton weight.

David Milner, 2010–Present

All-round good guy. Fantastic workhorse. Well educated and intelligent. Always willing to learn. Currently the highest-placed player still playing in the Premier League, who, when scores, is never on the losing side. There must be something wrong with him. Oh, yeah, he doesn't touch alcohol.

Costel Pantillimon, 2011–14

So tall, it is reputed to be 2 degrees cooler and somewhat damper around his head; obviously this is not a good thing when living in Manchester, as proved when he buggered off, sick of being afflicted with a damp patch.

Mario Balotelli, 2011–13

There are crazy people, really crazy people, and then there is Mario Balotelli. Hatter, March hare, or brush even. Mario is all of them wrapped up into one awesome person and that's before we even get to his off-field antics. The author of this book hopes he runs for world president one day, because he'd definitely get his vote.

Samir Nasri, 2011–Present
It was said by Arsenal fans that Nasri moved to Manchester City for money and money only; he proved this point by winning a couple of Premier League titles, the Football League Cup and the FA Community Shield.

Sergio Agüero, 2011–Present
Proving that not all Argentinian strikers are alike, Agüero has the added bonus of being a part of Diego Maradona's family – thankfully though, it isn't a blood relationship, but it was always useful to have Diego around when Mario occasionally behaved himself. Oh, he's rather good at that kicky football thing, too; Messi says so.

Steven Jovetić, 2013–Present
Manchester City's very own invisible man, to the point fans were beginning to wonder if Jovetić even existed. They discovered he very much did exist when he kept taking off all his clothes every time he scored.

A Manchester City Fan of the ADUG Era Has His Say

Name: Simon Cork
Age: 23
First City game ever attended: Never been.

Oh, we are the greatest in the land! Where were you when you were shit?

Huh? What's that? Nah, mate, I'm blue through and through. City shirt? Umm … it's in the wash, mate … yeah, that's it, it's in the wash.

We are City, and we'll score when we want! Yeah, City are great aren't they? Always have been, too. Do I know what? The history? No, why should I? It's all about today, isn't it? Although that time we got beat by Sunderland – what was that about? We should be beating them like 8-0, or something! What do we pay all these players millions for? They're all crap.

Favourite players? Umm ... lemme think a moment ... well, I always like to see Agüero, Tevez, and Robinho line up together; that's awesome that is. Barcelona? Aspire to be like them? We're better than them! We would beat any team in the world, every day of the week!

What? You don't agree? And you call yourself a City fan? Look, I gotta go. Huh? City are playing today? They are? Oh, well, I've made plans. Maybe next time, yeah?

Notable Managers

Steve Coppell, 7 October 1996–8 November 1996
Steve Coppell came to the club in 1996, with the fans hoping he could bring success to the team. He lasted thirty days. In charge for only six games, with two wins, three losses and one draw, he is to-date City's third most successful manager, and seventh longest serving one.

Malcolm Allison, 7 October 1971–30 March 1973
'Yes, I had a good shag this morning. Now let's get down to some bloody good football, shall we?'

Frank Clark, 29 December 1997–17 February 1998
'They're out to get me!'

Kevin Keegan, 24 May 2001–11 March 2005
'Defenders? No, sorry, I'm not following you.'

John Benson, 3 February 1983– 7 June 1983
'So, it's 3 points for a win now, is it? Why was I not told about this before?'

Wilf Wild, 14 March 1932–1 December 1946
'It's only the bloody Luftwaffe! Now get out on that pitch!'

No One, 12 March 2005–20 March 2005
'I'm not really here.'

Tom Maley, July 1902–July 1906
'Buck ye, FA, ye cannae keep City doon, nae matter hoo much ye try!'

Alan Ball, 30 June 1995–26 August 1996
'No, I have never met my best friend Francis Lee before in my life.'

Tony Book, 23 October 1973–22 November 1973, 12 April 1974–16 July 1979, 9 October 1980–16 October 1980, 29 November 1989–5 December 1989, 27 August 1993 3 p.m.– 4.45 p.m.
'Why they didn't ask me when they threw Bobby Manc out, I do not know; it's not like I wasn't there anyway, was it?'

Who?	Why They Were Great	Why They Were Not So Great	Best Position	Actual Position
Joey Barton	English, so could always be sold for an inflated price. Actually quite a good footballer.	Football tended to come second to minor things such as GBH and setting fire to other players.	Centre of midfield.	Cell block B-6. Lights out!
Carlos Tevez	So good he merely had to look at the ball to cause it to go in the back of the net.	After seven years in England, the only English he knew was the word 'no'.	Lone striker.	Risco Plateado Golf Club.
Billy Meredith	Way ahead of his time in terms of footballing skill.	Was always the first to complain. Liked a bet.	Out and out striker.	Playing for Manchester United.
Fred Tilson	In terms of goalscoring ability, he was the Carlos Tevez of the day.	If there was a bone in his body yet to be broken, it was already on his to-do list.	Up front.	Wing D of Tameside General.
Rodney Marsh	Holding up the ball.	Holding up the ball.	Attacking midfielder.	On Twitter pissing off City fans.
Paul Lake	Sheer brilliance. Labelled as the next Bobby Moore.	Played about as much as Bobby Moore did in the early 1990s.	Anywhere he wanted, as far as this author is concerned.	Cheapest chop-shop Swales could find.
Richard Dunne	Man mountain, never afraid to get into the thick of the action. Occasionally scored, too. Did wonders for kid's cereal.	Goals were generally at the wrong end of the pitch.	Central defence.	Head in hands, after 'scoring' again.
Shaun Goater	Looked useless, but was in fact completely the exact opposite.	He left.	Up front.	Running circles around Gary Neville.
David White	Immense pace, brought about City's much heralded and feared counter-attacking football.	Had Brian Horton as a manager.	Right-wing.	Travelling back in time, due to the speed he was running.
Neil Young	Tended to score in lots of important games, so was crucial to our continuing successes …	… Which we discovered when he left in 1972.	Attacking winger.	Getting an even better goal to game ratio after leaving us.
Georgie Kinkladze	He was just damn good at football.	Had a tendency to keep the ball and lose it after running past the fifth defender in a row, or pass to a team-mate and then they lost it to the first defender.	Anywhere with the ball at his feet.	Somewhere on the pitch, wondering why he hasn't got the ball.
Glauber Berti	We had to wait an entire season to witness his awesomeness.	He basically did nothing, save for giving a throw-in away.	Left-back *v.* Bolton Wanderers.	It isn't called a Berti for nothing, y'know.

THE FUTURE

It didn't take too long for the project at Manchester City to be widely regarded as how to do things right, although it certainly helped that the Manchester Council basically bent over, grabbed the back of their calves and said 'Do what you want.'

City had gone from 'Manchester who?' to the one all others across the world looked up to, whether it be on or off the field. Everything about the club was heralded as a success, even to the extent that Moonchester is now the fourth most recognisable character on Earth.

Manchester itself changed completely once ADUG had built everything they wanted to around the vastly expanded stadium – it had to, because as one council official commented: 'The rest of the city just looks shit now; we'll have to do something about that.' What was once the most famous industrialized city on the planet, and then home to the Madchester scene, was now a footballing mecca. Well, for one team at any rate.

The stock market crash of 2018 hit Manchester United PLC hard and within three seasons they had plummeted into the Championship under the tutelage of player-manager Ryan Giggs, who had returned back from hanging up his boots (he so wants that magic number of 1,000 League games played). While that was bad enough for them, in 2022 the European Super League came into effect, brought in earlier than expected because of the crash; Manchester United have now not played in Europe for over twenty years.

The Premier League did survive, as did all the top-flight European leagues, as they proved to be of a more level playing field, primarily because everyone in them was crap.

A City Fan of the Good-Time 2030s Has His Say

Name: David 72967
Age: 17 per cent of life spent
First City game ever attended: Physically or metaphysically?

I was reading something the other day that said Manchester City used to be just a football club. I know! How archaic is that? Oh, when was it now? ... 2029? When City were recognized by the UN and got a seat on the National Security Council. Yeah, what a day that was! I got my residency of The Kingdom of Etihad a couple of years ago and have never looked back.

Of course, things don't always go our way; second in the League at the moment with Barcelona hot on our tails three points behind. But we've hit a good run of form, so you never know we might yet catch up with Chesterfield.

Favourite moment? That's a toughie because there's been so many. Oh, you remember the earthquake of 2027? That finally answered the question of what would happen if everyone in China jumped up and down at once. The Chinese Government banned the Poznan after that. Shame really.

Who? Manchester United? No, sorry, never heard of 'em. Hang on ... call incoming. What, now? But I'm in the middle of some interview thing. OK, I'll be there in 10 minutes, alright?

Sorry, my kid brother says there's some trouble at the office. S'pose I'd better get going, there's a 216 shuttle bus arriving in 3 minutes. Gotta love them earth-to-lunar services – see ya laters.

Alternatively…

As my mother always used to tell me as a kid: 'If you're going to do something, at least do it properly,' and so if you have been a City fan for a good number of years, you know that when things go bad they can go real bad; City have never done things by halves.

This is true for the alternate future history of the club, or, as Manchester United fans call it, 'hopefully will happen very soon'.

However, for things to go bad now it would have to be on an apocalyptic scale, such as everything east of Italy and west of Pakistan being swallowed by a black hole, or the world experiencing the Second Coming of Jesus (obviously he would have a City season ticket, as it would be 'My Dad's own club'). Either that or Peter Swales returns from the dead.

What we do know for a fact is that even if any of these events took place City fans would still turn up in their thousands; it's who we are. Undoubtedly, going to away games would be a little easier, as most (if not all) of them would be placed under the heading of 'get yourself a No. 216 bus timetable'. It would also be much cheaper to go to matches, which is nothing to be sniffed at – in your face Premier League 2034 prices of £409 per class-C game.

Of course there will be some who would long for the current players of the day to have the talent of Danny Mills or even Christian Negouai, but, for the most of us, it would be like reliving the 1890s, where you could meet the centre-forward at The Butcher's Arms in Droylsden and buy him a pint or two, or give the first-choice 'keeper a ride to the ground because he is already four times over the legal limit.

Mind you, if all this does happen, I will buy the club using the proceeds from this book, and yes, we will buy Macclesfield's excellent left-back to shore up our defence.

A City Fan of the Not-So-Good-Time 2030s Has His Say

Name: Zach Wichert
Age: 42
First City game ever attended: Sometime in the 2010s

Me Dad used to always say, God rest his soul, that he missed the real football – y'know when we were shit and playing in the lower divisions. If only we were that good now! Have you seen that centre-forward we got? I don't think he even touched the ball during the last game, mind you it was funny when he thought he'd scored running off celebrating only to find out it was his boot that came off and went in.

All went wrong? Well, it was after ADUG left us, wasn't it? Went into administration six times in a row – there's another record we now hold. By the time it was all over Hyde FC were offering us a charity match to raise funds. Mind you, the fans now own the club; got a hundred shares myself – only cost me 47c, with postage of EU$16.85.

Hopes? You're having a laugh, aren't ya? Hopes can destroy a man's soul; you just gotta take what comes and accept it.

Next match? Wouldn't miss it! It's the derby! I do hope we knock a few past FC United – should be a cracking game.

But I am blue through and through, and always will be – it's in my blood y'see ... well, that and some radiation poisoning.

City 'Til I Die!

The Manchester City Fan's Contract

I hereby declare myself as a fan and supporter of Manchester City and therefore I am legally obliged to perform, or adhere to, the following:

I.   My love for the club knows no bounds, much like the other important things in my life, such as alcohol, women/men (cross out where applicable), sleeping and occasionally saying dumb things.

II. Whosoever wears the sky blue of my club, and enters the field of play, will garner my support, even if I am of the understanding that said player is a complete and utter tool (please see clause 1 for further clarification).

III. Even if I was not a Manchester City fan, when we were beaten 2-1 by Lincoln City away all those many (blue) moons ago, I will endeavour to learn how crap we have been in the past, thereby realizing how awesome we are today and therefore how grateful I am.

IV. I will realize that Colin Bell was the greatest ever Manchester City player and that entering into discussion as to a possible alternative is forbidden.

V.   I understand that money does not equal success, although recognizing that it sure as hell bleedin' helps.

VI. A 1-0 win amounts to the same points as a 5-4 win and so I will not expect that every scoreline will make it look like Kevin Keegan is back in charge.

VII. Where the signee is a heterosexual male, man-love for David Silva is perfectly acceptable.

VIII. Where the signee is a heterosexual female, the same law applies to Moonbeam.

IX. I am of the understanding that my sworn enemy is Manchester United, but that I have far better things to do with my time (bathroom visits being a prime example) than have a go at them, unless of course an opportunity arises that is simply too good to turn down.

X.   I will accept that on occasion Manchester City will do strange things, and that this is perfectly normal behaviour for my club.

XI. I will learn all the words to the masterpiece that was 'The Boys in Blue' sung by the Manchester City squad of the 1970s.

XII. Even though Manchester City is God's own club, we do not believe we have a divine right to win everything. This is a trait of being a fan of Manchester United, which has a devil on its crest for a good reason.

XIII. Doing the Poznan is acceptable only immediately after a goal has been scored, otherwise you just look silly.

XIV. Having a sense of humour is a legal requirement.

XV. I will accept that many in the media are numpties and do not want Manchester City to succeed, so the louder they shout the better we are doing. Encourage the shouting.

Clause 1: Law II, could, and can, be dismissed in good faith, in the case of Joey Barton.

Signature   ....

Date   ....

Whiteboard Answers

1. Frank Clarke
2. Stuart Pearce
3. Kevin Keegan
4. Sven Gorän Eriksson and the Middlesbrough match
5. Manuel Pellegrini
6. Roberto Mancini

Where Did I Get All This Information From, and Why Is There Not More of It in This Book?

When I sat down to write this book, I started making notes – lots and lots of notes – and I was surprised at exactly how much I knew. I may not have known who the second scorer of City's goal away at Carlisle United in 1966 was (it was Pardoe by the way, thanks Wikipedia), but I knew obscure facts such as the date of our very first match and that Les McDowell cost £7,000. But how did I know this? I read. A lot. And spent an awfully long time discussing City's history with other Blues in the pub.

Over the years, the writings of Gary James, Ian Penney, autobiographies of past players, match reports, and countless pages in the dark recesses of the internet had stuck in my brain (this is presumably why there is now no room in there to remember things like birthdates, and what I should have picked up at the grocery store).

Of course, when it came to specific dates and such like, I did have to turn to the internet and these authors to check when something had happened. They had all come before me and knew their stuff, and maybe one day someone will turn to this book to check up on something that they already knew but was a bit hazy on the exact details, only to then realise that what I wrote probably wasn't true.

Too many Blues don't know about our history, but hopefully this book has taught you a few things (and made you laugh) and now you want to learn more. And that is the answer – you must read (particularly James and Penney). Knowledge is power (although I cannot be held accountable if you, too, also end up forgetting to buy toothpaste).

As for why this book isn't bigger, I wanted it to be an easy read, and while I could have gone into far more detail, there are many of you who either do not have the time or simply do not wish to sit down with something that has more pages than a telephone directory. Maybe one day I will update this book and add in far more.

Again, hopefully, you've enjoyed this most tongue-in-cheek tone and it will make you read other (serious) writings.

Thanks

Mike Devlin

P.S. That one real direct word-for-word quote I mentioned at the very beginning? It was from Manchester Council after I asked them about where all the City player roads have gone to – I wasn't best pleased with their answer. All the other quotes are not real.

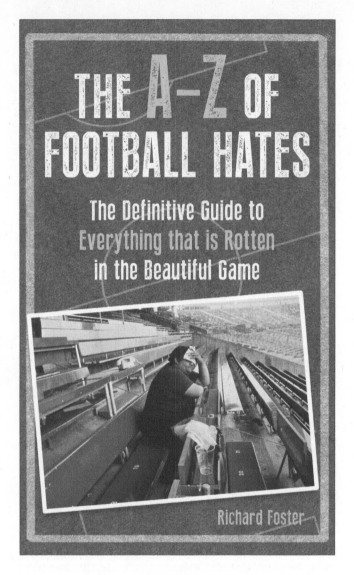